contents

styles of learning

Left brain	Right brain
are you organised?	do you do things on the spur of the moment?
are you analytical?	are you intuitive?
does the clock rule your life?	are you often late?
do you make lists of things you have to do?	do you do things when they occur to you rather than in a fixed order?
are you a worrier?	are you very easy going?
are you a planner?	are you a daydreamer?

It might seem odd to start a book about the use of ICT to support learners with dyslexia with a quiz – and one which is not scientifically valid and which is not by any stretch of the imagination a formative assessment. Nevertheless, it may help you to understand that some children and adults work differently and seem to think in a way that the rest of us find odd and sometimes frustrating.

We think, "If only they did things like us, they'd soon get the hang of it", but they don't, and often can't, do things the way we do and this is where the problem lies.

In 1981 Roger Sperry won the Nobel Peace Prize for his research on left-brain and right-brain hemisphere brain functions. He discovered that most of us use both sides of our brain but have a bias to one side or the other. Traditional academia is very left brained with an emphasis on words, details, and categorising. The right side of the brain focuses on non-verbal and intuitive ways of working.

If you answered yes to most of the questions in the left-hand column, you are probably a left-brained person, which means that the left hemisphere is the dominant one. The left-brain hemisphere specialises in logical, analytical and linear thinking and offers a very verbal approach to information. If the right-hand column describes you more accurately, then the right brain hemisphere is probably dominant and this specialises in intuitive, perceptual and non-linear thinking.

Being left or right brained is neither an advantage nor a drawback. In some ways it is rather like being left-handed. However, it has implications for the way people learn, the strategies they need to develop and the way we can use computers and software to support them.

According to Sperry, if children have difficulty learning to tell the time, following instructions which involve left and right, learning the alphabet or anything which has to be remembered in sequence, they may well be right brained. They are likely to be artistic and creative but disorganised at times.

> Sean likes to have written directions to get from one part of town to another. If faced with a map he translates it into sentences, "Turn right into Cole Street, second left and first right." Pablo prefers maps to find his way: he loses the sequence of verbal instructions and gets lost but he has an almost photographic memory for maps and a really good sense of direction.

Left brain characteristics	Right brain characteristics
language	images
rules and grammar	awareness of shape
numbers	appreciation of patterns
sequences	ability to work in three dimensions
linearity	rhythm and musical appreciation
analysis	seeing the whole picture

It is suggested that many learners with dyslexia have right-brain dominance. They find that the range of subjects and the style of teaching in school do not play to their strengths and can leave them with a sense of frustration and failure. However, the best multimedia programmers may be right brained too: they are able to operate in non-linear ways and see patterns and links which are not apparent to left-brained individuals.

It is important that as teachers we do not always follow the deficit model. Because someone is dyslexic, it certainly does not mean that they are unintelligent. Sometimes we are just not clever enough to see where their strengths lie. It is easy to see the problems. These may include difficulties with any – or all – of the following:

- reading
- spelling
- sequencing
- left and right
- visual or auditory discrimination and perception
- pronunciation, particularly words of three or more syllables
- long-term and short-term memory
- organisation – ranging from planning to being in the right place at the right time.

You will see that most of their problems are based on a right-brain model of what we expect of a learner. We are not, for example, measuring the ability to perceive patterns or rhythm, at which they may excel. In addition some learners exhibit:

- memory deficits
- slowness in information processing
- visual and spatial deficits
- planning and organisational difficulties
- difficulty in initiating action, or lack of motivation
- loss of confidence and poor self-image.

Some of these characteristics are not innate, they have occurred as a consequence of poor learning techniques or a history of failure. Learners may have memory deficits because they are being asked to learn by rote instead of creating mind maps; they may lack motivation and become passive because they have no experience of success. The problems are not restricted to text and language activities. In mathematics we see learners struggle to learn tables and recall number bonds. Often these are difficult because they rely on memory and sequencing. We need to pay more attention to the strategies which work for individual students and be prepared to set aside our prejudices. "If they just put in the effort to learn their tables off by heart, they would find it so much easier," we think. Here we are working from *our* perspective, often a left-brain view of how to absorb information.

Similarly, Dr Steve Chinn of Mark College, a specialist dyslexia centre in Somerset, has identified different learning styles in the field of mathematics. He has described them as 'Inchworm' and 'Grasshopper' styles.

Inchworm	Grasshopper
focuses on parts and details	holistic – goes for an overview
looks at numbers to choose the right rules and formulae	looks at numbers to estimate an answer
sticks to one method	tries a variety of approaches
works in a logical structured way	works back from trial answer
uses exact numbers	rounds up and down and adjusts numbers to get answers
is reliant on pencil and paper	prefers mental arithmetic approaches
works in structured steps	'plucks numbers out of air'

S.J. Chinn and J.R. Ashcroft, *Mathematics and dyslexia: A Teaching Handbook*, Whurr, 1998

In order to be a successful mathematician, a learner needs both approaches at different times. Dyslexic learners can be found in both categories. Dyslexic inchworms stick to tried and tested methods which rely on memory so they often experience little success. Grasshoppers, on the other hand, experiment more with numbers and may make quite good progress until they are forced to document their working in examinations.

We are beginning to appreciate that there are all sorts of ways of learning information: some people use words, some use pictures, others use mnemonics – to learn colours of the rainbow, for example. If we take spellings as an example, some people learn the word *necessary* by splitting it nec-ess-ary. Others concentrate of the 'cess' part and link it to a 'cess pit' waiting to trap the poor speller, while others visualise a shirt and remember that it has 1 collar and 2 sleeves. These are all acceptable ways of working and no one way is The Correct One, so it helps if we and the learner can find a way of working that suits their learning style.

Much effort has been spent on analysing the spelling, punctuation and handwriting of learners with dyslexia. As well as considering the visual and auditory nature of spelling errors, we must look for patterns in successful spellings so we can find out what works and build on that. We also need to consider attitude and motivation, for they play an important part in a learner's willingness to revise his or her work.

With its ever-increasing range of software, ICT offers help to the dyslexic learner, in diagnosis and assessment of the problem and in the programs which support the development of skills. In the chapters which follow, we look at the strategies and software which ICT can provide.

why use a computer?

[handwritten margin note: Learning - active - Constructivism]

The only way to learn many things in life is to do them and learn from our mistakes. Unfortunately, for many thousands of students in the education system today, the mistakes are so acute that the only lesson they learn is that they are failures.

Many people find writing hard work: what are we going to write? How should we start? Does this sound right? Is it in the right order? How will we sum up at the end? Most of us compose in sentences in paragraphs and check the individual words afterwards. For those with dyslexia, each word is a hurdle and for some each letter requires a concentrated effort.

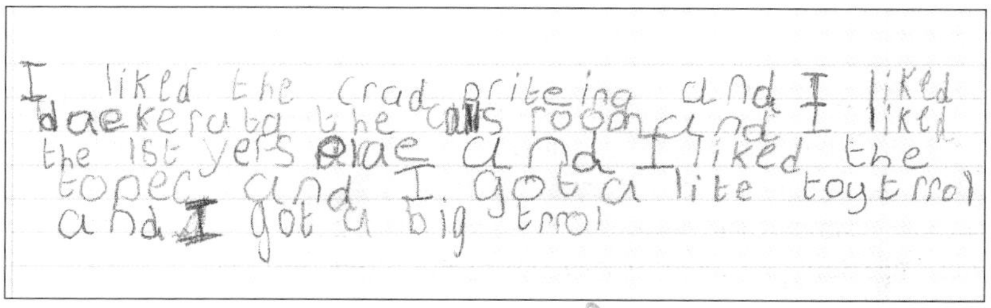

> I liked the crad oriteing and I liked daekerubg the cals roomand I liked the 1st yers rlae and I Iliked the topec and I got a lite toy tmol and I got a big tmol

Look at the sample of writing on the left. It is by Adrian, aged 10. He is writing about what he enjoyed in the school's Christmas activities. The handwriting and spelling are poor, the syntax is rambling, the ideas are under-developed and the vocabulary is very basic.

Technology can break down the barriers by making the task manageable. If you have access to a keyboard you don't have to recall the letters: they are all in front of you. You do not have to worry about legibility and you do not ruin your work with crossings out because you can delete or amend a word or phrase as you go. Technology is the great leveller: once typed, a passage could have been written by a six-year-old with poor motor skills or by a prolific novelist. No one can make judgements based on the appearance of the work; instead they look at the content, the style and the message. Not only that, it is harder to lose written work from a computer than it is to lose a piece of paper and for students who have difficulties organising themselves, this may be a serious consideration. For coursework, it is important that the work is kept safely and is legible. At the very least, technology can help with these modest demands.

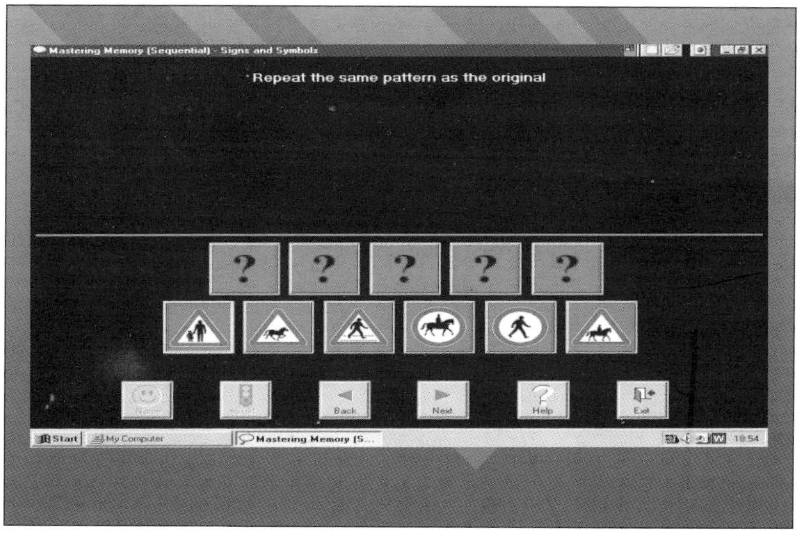

[handwritten margin notes: 2:3:11, presentation, content + style, judged, Organisation]

There are now several software programs which can help with the process of identifying strengths and weaknesses. CoPS Baseline Assessment is a piece of software designed to assess children when they enter school. It is quick and easy to use once staff are trained and produces reports which show a child's individual strengths and learning needs.

Poor short-term memory can be one of the factors which affects the learning performance. In addition, it may manifest itself as behaviour or attention deficit problems in the mainstream classroom. As the learners cannot remember the task/word/instructions properly, they develop strategies for getting round the problem and act as the class clown.

A sequencing task from Mastering Memory

Mastering Memory, a program from CALSC, isn't an assessment and it isn't a game. Based on the work of Buzan and Feuerstein, it teaches people a range of strategies to improve their auditory and visual memory. The aim is to help people learn strategies to improve their memory and to build on their strengths as well. Research shows that after learning strategies such as rehearsing and repeating sequences, learners can improve both their long- and short-term memory which means that their time in the classroom will be more productive.

Another useful program from CALSC is Timely Reminders, based on the thinking of Buzan and Ebbinghaus, which teaches strategies for improving memory and thereby enhancing the learning process. It is a framework which manages the process of reviewing things so learners start to organise, review and revisit their work regularly as a means of refreshing their memory and learning more effectively.

A new program from iANSYST which has received considerable praise is Wordswork. Designed for secondary and adult learners with dyslexia, it uses an interactive approach to study skills. It covers subjects as diverse as essay writing, revision, handwriting and time management.

The AcceleRead, AcceleWrite program, which uses special cards and a talking word processor, is an excellent tool for learners in Key Stages 2–4 for improving short-term memory (and keyboarding and spelling too). The learner has to read a short phonic sentence from a card, remember it, repeat it, type it into a talking word processor, listen to it and then check to see if the sentence is the same as the original. In doing so, the learner has to:

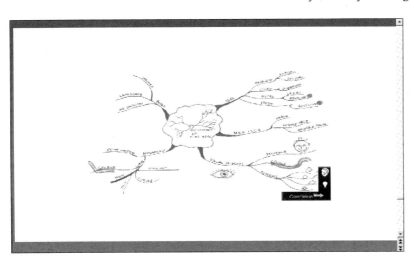

Mind mapping from Wordswork

- read
- remember
- repeat
- type
- listen
- reflect.

A project in Somerset which used the Talking Pendown word processor was very successful (details of the scheme can be found on the iANSYST Web site). After six hours' tuition, the first group showed amazing increases in their skills which were maintained over a full year.

Skill	Mean increase (months)
word recognition	8.3
spelling	4.1
auditory short-term memory	15.3

Results of *Somerset Talking Word Processor Project*

You need to be aware, however, that the sentences that cover the spelling patterns on the cards are unconnected with each other and some are somewhat bizarre, which can cause problems for young children or those still operating at a concrete level. However, the teaching technique is valid for all children, and shorter sentences made up by the teacher or taken from a reading book, can be used to good effect with younger children.

In the next section, we look more closely at using ICT to support the writing process.

dyslexia and writing

Gary is seven years old. He has some co-ordination problems. He frequently has his shoes on the wrong feet, sometimes holds his pencil in his right hand, sometimes in his left. He has serious problems with reading and a real block about writing. He has yet to complete more than two or three lines of writing, quite often misspells his name and most of the words he writes are all but unrecognisable.

Rachel has dreadful handwriting, poor spelling and an attitude. She seems determined to get the school to exclude her. On the odd occasions that a subject interests her, she is quite good at explaining things to her teachers and seems to have a good understanding of the subjects that she likes, but it is uphill work.

Diane has recently completed a degree. "As a first-year student, I was having difficulties coping with the course. I was having problems with spelling and grammar in written assignments, difficulties in understanding the requirements of examination and assignment questions. Sometimes I would misread the text and lose the meaning of what was written."

there is no such thing as a typical dyslexic learner

With the reluctant dyslexic writer, sentences are short, words are simplistic and the reader is left with a feeling that the effort of writing has driven out the desire to communicate. Sometimes they seem overwhelmed by the blank page or blank screen. Some, like Rachel, would rather not try because that way they cannot fail. The disorganised writer, in contrast, finds difficulty in focusing. The text goes on and on, rambling from episode to episode as if quantity rather than quality is the determining factor.

some ideas for encouraging writing

working from pictures and sounds:

- choose a picture to label
- listen to music and write the words and phrases that come into your mind
- create captions for a photo story.

work as a pair:

- type a conversation
- type jokes
- write a section of a branching story.

Collaborative writing, writing frames, planning tools, postcards and post-its can all be used to encourage the reluctant or disorganised writer. Write notes on little pieces of paper. Better still, let the planning stage be in the form of drawings or symbols and move them round on the table so that the learner is working in a more holistic way and not always using linear structures. Use Inspirations, Expression, Thinksheet or some other mind-mapping tool.

Get learners to talk about what the work will be like and better still, to record their ideas on tape both as a prompt and as evidence of the planning process. Perhaps the learner will need help to get a draft onto paper. It might be that someone else types up the first draft from a taped account or that the learner is given a scaffold on which to build.

Writing frames can also be useful in this context. These contain structured phrases which characterise particular genres such as formulating an argument or describing a process. Word Bar has examples of this, as shown below.

With suitable support at this stage, the learner can make enormous progress. Instead of focusing on transcription, the learner can move to editing, where so much learning takes place. Editing involves more than re-arranging writing. It involves reviewing and evaluating, comparing what is on the screen, or on the print-out, with the vision in the writer's head. It is important to concentrate on the flow of the words rather than difficulties in decoding so, where there are problems, use a screen reader or talking word processor to read back the text, or read it aloud to the learner.

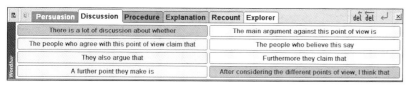

An example of writing frames as shown in Word Bar

Even with a fairly sketchy outline, it's often worth printing out the first attempt. This encourages the student because it makes their efforts more concrete. Where the ideas are very disjointed, you can mark different sections in different colours or underline all the information about one person/theme so the writer can see what needs to be linked together. Try to keep drafts as a record of the progress of the writing, as this can be a useful motivator for the learner, showing how a few key words have been expanded into a longer piece of text. Make notes on the print-out, highlighting important bits in one colour, gaps in the story line in another. Draw arrows to show where text needs to be moved about.

It is easier to edit the surface of the text (the spelling, punctuation and layout), than the meaning. However, if we want learners to develop their writing skills, we must encourage them to take a critical view of the content. You need to show them that editing is much more than a proof-reading exercise. If you stick to spelling, then the learner will too.

If you start by emphasising the positive, it's less painful when you move on to the weaker parts. "Show me the bit you like best" will highlight the aspect the learner thinks is most important, and can be expanded by asking, "Can we say something about what his coat/car/house looked like?".

Where a pupil has a limited vocabulary or leans too heavily on stock phrases, you can use the 'find' facility to highlight all the occurrences of one word and then search for alternatives (a word processor's thesaurus may be helpful here too). Remember, adding information is less painful than removing it, and a word processor can facilitate the moving, copying and deleting of text until the writer is satisfied. You could also save different versions of the same text and compare them on screen. A screen reader will enable the learner to hear individual words (for spelling) and whole sentences (for punctuation).

As more homes have suitable computers, much of this work can be done in small, daily stints at home, which provide the necessary remediation support. This also reduces the time the child needs to be withdrawn from lessons. To be effective, however, requires good home–school liaison, so that work done at home links with strategies that are being developed in school. For children who do not have access to a computer at home, school lunch-time and homework clubs may provide an alternative.

what can the computer offer?

For some people the task of handwriting recognisable letters in straight lines is such hard work, demanding concentration and mental energy, that there is none available for the task of deciding what to write. Some dyspraxic writers have dreadful handwriting: it is disjointed, spidery, fluctuating in size and hard to read – even by them. Others may have very neat writing, but if they make deep indentations through several pages and are constantly breaking pencil points and even pencils, they may have unrecognised dyspraxia. They have to put a great deal of physical effort and concentration into producing their neat writing, which leads to criticism by teachers when they produce less written work than would be expected from their oral ability.

The use of a keyboard can make a positive difference. Press a key and a well formed letter appears, the words are legible and in a straight line. AbilityNet (http:\\www.abilitynet.co.uk), an organisation which has done a considerable amount of work on improving access to computers for many groups of learners, suggests some of the following may be useful for learners with dyslexia who are using computers.

some simple ways of adapting a computer

Big, bright letters on keys: these sometimes help people to find the keys more quickly and with less effort. For some, they seem to 'cut through' difficulties in recognising and locating the right letter. They can be stuck on to the keys of any keyboard.

Big, bold upper-case key-tops: in yellow/black or white/black, these are available from Techno-vision systems, 76 Bunting Road Industrial Estate, Northampton, tel. 0164 79277. They cost around £15.

Lower-case alphabetical letters, yellow/black: these are available from Inclusive Technology, tel. 01457 819790. They cost around £5 for 5 sheets.

Larger letters: these can prove helpful, even when vision is not a problem. Letter size can be varied by changing the 'font' size or, in some word processors, by using a 'zoom' facility. It may even be that the differences in appearance between one font or type style and another can be important. Try some alternatives.

Double spacing: for some people this can help a great deal (but remember o put the whole document back to single spacing before you print it). Your manual, or on-screen help, should help you find out how to try these ideas.

You also need to consider how word processing can increase the readability of text for hand-outs and other materials. With the advent of word processing and desktop publishing, staff have started to be far more adventurous when creating hand-outs. Desktop publishing and the more sophisticated word processors enable writers to make text bold or italic, enlarge headings, develop style sheets and incorporate graphics. One of the problems is that most users have had no training in typography or graphics and may inadvertently make materials harder to read.

Justified text (with straight margins at both left and right, like newspaper columns) is more difficult to read because the computer alters the distance between words to make the line lengths match. This can give the impression of rivers running down the page, and make it difficult for learners to develop rhythmical eye movements when scanning the page.

Layout and presentation affect readability. The choice of type style or font and the spacing both between letters and between words can alter the learner's ability to read back what he or she has written. Allowing learners to experiment with different layouts heightens their awareness of the ways they can control the presentation of their work. For learners who find writing difficult, comparing different fonts and colour combinations on screen and on paper gives opportunities for decision-making and pride in the ownership of their work. Software in which text appears on screen in the same layout and type style as the printed version is helpful here.

Research by Dr Rosemary Sassoon demonstrated that eight-year-olds preferred typefaces with the plainness of san serif ascenders and descenders rather than the little feet put on the letters by designers of serif fonts. The children also liked letters that slanted. Distance between letters and also between words had a significant effect on ease of reading. These conclusions led Dr Sassoon to design a typeface specifically for children.

Older students with dyslexia who do not have access to Sassoon on their word processor often choose to use Arial, Comic Sans or Helvetica fonts.

This is an example of Comic Sans. It has a stylish look to it and is very uncluttered.

Many students have problems reading black print on white paper. It may be a good idea to use coloured paper for hand-outs. If this is impractical, it is worth remembering that some learners have benefited from using a coloured sheet of acetate laid over the page. A group of adult students who used this technique found yellow and green overlays the most effective but it is worth experimenting as people respond to different colours. They found they could work for much longer without getting tired and tutors noticed that they rubbed their eyes much less frequently. One learner reported that the acetate made 'the page go flat' because the page usually looked curved to him. Younger students have spoken of letters 'dancing' or the paper curving as they try to focus.

Because a screen is lit from behind and the contrast is better than on paper, some people find their reading and proof-reading skills are more accurate when they are editing on-line rather than from a print-out. With many packages, students can experiment with the background and foreground colours and with Windows 95

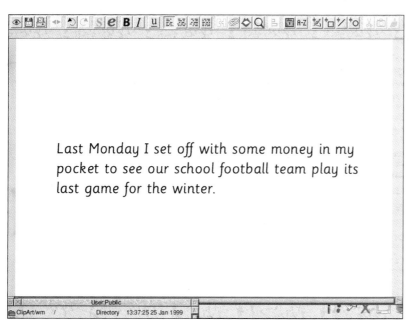

An example of the Sassoon typeface

Last Monday I set off with some money in my pocket to see our school football team play its last game for the winter.

it is possible to have all sorts of colour combinations. Emma's comments highlight the difference the colours and fonts can make:

> "I have a problem with eye sensitivity – certain colours can cause pain and discomfort to a dyslexic Although many word-processing packages allow you to change the colour of the text and the page, often this facility does not extend to spell checkers. Similarly there is often no choice of fonts for a spell checker. This may not seem a problem but my last piece of work was 1260 words in length and it took one hour and twenty minutes to spell check it. The point size was 10 and the font was not the one that I would have chosen. This made the process of spell checking even more time consuming than normal."

the power of word processing

When students use a word processor, they tend to write more because it is less of an effort. They can alter a piece of text time and again without having to rewrite or retype the parts that are right. Once they start to edit their work, students can become addicted to changing, altering and improving their text. This puts them in control. Whether they want to correct spellings as they go along or wait till the end and run a spell checker over the whole document, it's their decision.

Because the word processor minimises spelling and handwriting problems, students are free to concentrate on the ideas and the way they want to express them. This encourages them to be more adventurous in their use of language and syntax.

James (see left) is a fairly sophisticated user of text. What about people who are struggling to write more than a few lines? There are all sorts of tools which can benefit learners.

If they have a very limited spelling vocabulary, you might try packages which have a word bank or dictionary in their editing facilities. Students can call up the word bank by typing in the first letter or topic name and then choose the word they want.

Even more sophisticated is a predictive word processor, such as Co:Writer, PredictIT or Prophet. Originally devised for physically disabled students who might only be typing 10 letters a minute, these have now become very popular with many dyslexic writers. You need to know the first letter or sound and then the computer puts up a list of the most likely words. You can select a word, with one key press, or continue to write from the keyboard. These packages are particularly appropriate for students who have reading skills which are far more advanced than their writing or spelling.

Predictive word processors are grammatically quite sophisticated programs – Co:Writer from Don Johnson Software has more than 40,000 words in the main dictionary, for example. These can be adapted by adding prefixes or suffixes or new words can be added to the dictionary. Co:Writer understands many grammar rules such as verb tense, word relationships and subject-verb agreement so if I type *we*, it knows that *am* should not be on the list.

Prediction speeds up the physical process of writing and this seems to influence the composition process for writers with specific learning difficulties. Often it stimulates more adventurous syntax. For once, their writing can keep up with their thoughts and they can develop a flow of ideas, instead of groping for each letter while trying to remember what they want to say.

Voice recognition is another way of getting the words on the page (and covered in greater detail on page 14).

James is working towards GCSEs and feels he could not manage without a word processor for his coursework. He claims he would spend every weekend copying out versions of assignments and introducing new spelling errors with each new draft. For him the major benefits of word processing are:

- better spelling
- increased confidence
- time savings, as there is no need to retype.

He can also reorganise work easily and expand ideas without rewriting whole documents. As a result, he can be more experimental with work and try things out by saving new drafts of work.

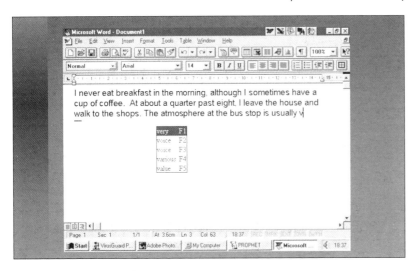

A pop-up window on a predictive word processor
– Prophet from the ACE Centre with Word

touch typing

Thomas is a Year 11 student in a mainstream secondary school. He has a severe specific learning difficulty and requires an amanuensis for nearly every piece of written work: "I have problems in all areas of school work... I have the words, I just cannot get them written down myself". Speech-recognition software had immediate appeal for Thomas and he was undaunted by the training and enrolment process.

He worked with the Learning Support Assistant daily and took delight in the control he achieved in producing work from his own hand (while acknowledging the computer's hand holding to do so!). He used continuous speech software on a stand-alone PC. He had patience and determination and was able to speak consistently, if not always clearly. He soon learnt how to train words which were not recognised and seemed to enjoy the mastery of these techniques.

Thomas had some computer skills and was willing to see that he and the computer were a partnership in the training process. His one distinct advantage over other students was his ability to dictate. He had been used to dictating to an amanuensis for a number of years and the skills he developed were invaluable to him as he gained confidence with using the software. He was soon able to work independently, and although he still experiences difficulties choosing the right words for correction, he has a new pride, raised self-esteem and the tool to work to produce text on his own for the first time.

The speech-recognition software has been so successful that it has now been installed on his home computer too. In Thomas's words: "It's like being given wings – you can just fly."

Within dyslexia circles there are many supporters of touch typing who can cite examples of children and adults who struggle to write the word *was* but remember that the letters form a triangle on the left-hand side of the keyboard. Other teachers feel that touch typing is an additional burden to impose on learners who are already struggling and finding that their homework takes hours to complete. On the other hand, some of the results are extremely interesting. Students learn finger patterns on the computer which reinforce correct spellings. They are looking and choosing, building up letter strings and words rather than worrying about the orientation of individual letters. In this way they are developing and practising skills while composing.

Some say extra burden

Perhaps the most useful feature of this way of working is that it enables older students to revisit phonics without loss of face. For those students who have not managed to link sound and symbol in a reliable way, this is a chance to start from scratch while learning a new skill which may improve their chances of employment.

There are many good typing tutors on the market. Type To Learn, from iANSYST, teaches students to type while reinforcing spelling, grammar, composition and punctuation skills.

Touch-type, Read and Spell is a computer program based on the Hornsby *Alpha to Omega* scheme which has provided a breakthrough for many students with dyslexic problems. All the vowels are learned first so that the learner is typing real words from the beginning. The screen can be customised to suit individual preferences. There is no negative feedback and nothing incorrect appears on screen. Touch-type, Read and Spell has over 600 short modules and some students manage 10 modules in a session.

No -ve feedback

The screen has a picture of a hand and shows which finger to use for the keys. A red star or a beep shows a mistake has been made and then the user has to correct it. There is no negative feedback and nothing incorrect appears on screen.

The whole programme is visual: a bar on the left of the screen records typing speed, a bar across the top shows how far through the exercise the student has got and a bar on the right gives a percentage for accuracy. Not only can students keep track of their progress but the tutor can see at a glance how they are getting on without having to home in and interrupt. If the tutor wants more detailed feedback he or she can consult the management system provided as part of the program. This records the module, speed, and accuracy as a series of statistics or as a graph, which makes it easier to spot trends.

Tutor can get feedback

An exercise from Type to learn

speech feedback and recognition

One of the most useful facilities a computer can offer is the use of speech feedback. Often this is synthetic, which has a tinny quality but which will read back anything that is written on screen. More modern packages offer a range of voices – male, female, child or robot. Some children who have been unwilling to commit their thoughts to paper enjoy the challenge of typing words for the computer to say.

Older readers can develop their skills by using specialised reading programs and learn to use a screen reader or talking word processor so they can access worksheets, e-mails and information from CD-ROM encyclopaedias and other resources.

Richard's spelling and handwriting are so poor that it is sometimes difficult to work out what he has written yet he expresses himself well orally and sometimes uses words that are very sophisticated and adult. We have been working on a phonic programme using a talking computer. He is just starting on blends and can now recognise initial phonics. The use of speech really has made a difference to his progress. He works from cards: he reads the sentence, says it, types it and listens to it. Not only does he get immediate feedback but also the speech seems to keep him on target and stop him getting distracted.

When she heard the text read back to her, she knew she wanted to change the wording. "I think I would have realised that I had over-used the word *hotel* but I didn't notice that I'd written *now* three times."

Robert was studying slavery for Key Stage 3 history. He is a statemented dyslexic learner and as well as his considerable writing difficulties, he finds reading a real chore. He had enjoyed discussions in class and the videos he had seen. When he went to the library, he quickly became discouraged as most of the books required good reading skills.

He found it particularly hard to use an index since, by the time he had worked through the alphabet, found the heading, noted the page number and started looking for the entry, he had forgotten what he wanted to know! His teacher showed him how to use the multimedia CD-ROM Africana. He had a go with the virtual tour of a slave port and then found articles he wanted. He highlighted them and copied them into Word. He listened to the information and decided what he wanted to keep and what could be deleted. He spent a long time editing the document and produced a long and detailed piece of work that showed his enthusiasm and considerable knowledge.

Where short-term memory causes a child to forget the beginning of a sentence before they get to the end, a talking word processor can provide a prompt by reading back what has already been written; an on-screen word/phrase grid can also provide useful prompting support.

Inclusive Writer combines many of these features. It offers audio support in picture/symbol annotations of words to help learners with poor reading and spelling skills, grids and word lists and speech support. All of these can be configured to get the right combination for a particular learner.

One of the best features of speech is that it gives instant feedback. Learners hear what they have written and this helps them to identify mistakes for themselves. Awareness of errors is the first step towards improving skills. The learner can hear the mistake and try alternatives or consult a spell checker. Sound is invaluable for those who confuse the letters *b* and *d*, for example, since they will often hear the difference when the word is read out.

Speech can also help in those cases where the learner has typed in the wrong word:

> Humphrey Bogart stared in Casablanca

Since *stared* is correctly spelt, it would not be picked up by a spell checker but the writer can hear that it is wrong. Some learners also find it helps them to become aware of repetitious phrasing in their work.

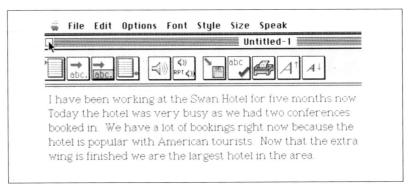

Using speech to listen to text in Write OutLoud

speech recognition

The other side to the coin of speech feedback is speech *input*. This is a system where, rather than inputting instructions to the computer via a keyboard or mouse, the computer responds to the user's voice. For learners with major problems of motor control or visual impairment, speech-recognition systems grant them access to computers which they could not otherwise use. Speech recognition has great potential for dyslexic learners, too, but learning to use it is no small undertaking.

There are two forms of speech-recognition software available. With *discrete* speech, you need to speak-one-word-at-a-time; with *continuous* speech, it's possible to speak naturally. The software can deal with regional accents, unclear speech and any number of irregularities, but it will need to be trained to do so and the user will need to be trained to speak consistently. Accuracy will improve over time, but it's important to select users with care, as they need to have:

- determination
- perseverance
- good initial training and support
- the desire and need to produce written text.

Speech-recognition software requires powerful hardware, although older machines will work with some of the earlier versions of speech-recognition software. Discrete software demands less from the hardware but still needs at least 64Mb of memory. The newest software versions require Pentium III machines with 128Mb of memory (for those who would just like it to run without technical tweaking!). These latest versions are able to run in both a continuous or discrete

Andrew has problems with reading, spelling and handwriting, and feels that his handwriting is his biggest obstacle. He had extremely high expectations of the speech-recognition software: this was going to be the answer to all his writing problems. He started with discrete speech software with the idea that he would move to a continuous system after a period of familiarisation.

The reality of the training and enrolment involved soon disillusioned him, however. He found it difficult to speak consistently, he raised his voice when recognition was poor and became frustrated and irritated by the resultant mistakes. He managed to establish a training routine, whereby his support assistant spoke the word and he repeated it, which worked well but allowed little scope for him to get on with much of his school work, unless it was discussed with him and prepared before the SR session. This proved far too time consuming and an added burden on Andrew's already overworked organisational skills.

He wanted to try continuous speech, but he lacked the dictation expertise. His voice, articulation and composition tailed away at the end of most sentences and he became even more disillusioned with the process. Andrew then decided that he would go back to discrete speech and try reading into it. Surprisingly, he persevered with this and began to become proficient at correction and started taking an interest in the layout of the work. Not only did he 'fuss with fonts', but because the software is very good at commands such as those for punctuation, it was noticeable that Andrew's written work began to benefit from the addition of punctuation.

He was not 'converted' to speech recognition as the aid that he hoped for, but there were incidental and added advantages for his reading, writing and computer skills. Andrew wants to be a tutor for other students who are starting to use the software, because he feels that he knows how they will feel and would be able to support them with training – a process which experience has shown to be very valuable for both.

mode and are consequently hungry for speed and memory. The learner's success is dependent on ease of use, so it's important to get the technology right.

You will also need to have the right microphone – noise cancellation microphones cope well with background noise and the voice of a trainer, helping with reading text to be input – and a high-quality sound card.

learning to use speech recognition

Every speech-recognition system needs to be trained to recognise the voice patterns of the user, and this can be very time consuming. The latest versions of software offer an almost pain-free process for enrolment, however, with the length of time much reduced and the interest and reading levels both wider and more appealing to children. It may be helpful to read the words and then ask the student to repeat them, or to choose a piece of software which offers that feature.

Putting your thoughts into words, speaking coherently and consistently may require considerable practice. The software takes for granted that the users will have the skills of dictation. This has been a major hurdle for some, but verbally adroit dyslexic students have managed with ease. For learners who have had to rely until now on the spoken word or dictating to an amanuensis, this software offers written text and independence.

Another useful tip is not to try to use all the features of the program straight away. As with most forms of sophisticated software, it probably has features that you will only need rarely, if at all. In the learning phase, it's not cheating to make a first draft with speech while the trainer edits using the keyboard. Many learners find it helpful to get used to a Dictaphone before they launch into speech-recognition systems.

Although recent software developments are able to cope with both discrete and continuous speech, which is a welcome and more natural approach, there has been success for a number of students whose thinking process has needed the more ponderous method offered by discrete speech. One student says, "It's more like writing, I have time to organise my thoughts". There is clearly an educational niche for both methods, if the combination does not lack any of the features of early discrete speech, and the future looks rosy, especially as desktop navigation, Internet and e-mail access look set to be voice activated.

You can find more information from the Becta Web site (www.becta.org.uk/projects/speechrecognition) or the Speaking to Write site at http://www.edc.org/spk2wrt/, which is an American project and a comprehensive site for users and trainers.

support tools

Spelling has been a major focus in the teaching of learners with specific learning difficulties for many years. There are many different strategies for the remediation of spelling problems. Some teachers like to analyse the learner's error patterns and then create a range of tailor-made exercises using programs such as Sherlock or GAMZ WordSearch from Inclusive Technology. Others prefer a structured program which is based on rules or letter patterns using software such as WordShark2, Eye for Spelling or Keyspell or Magic–e from Xavier.

Finding the right word with Wordshark2

Advocates of this approach point to the motivational qualities of computer-assisted learning, the patience and non-threatening aspects of being tutored by the machine. The ability to tailor programs to the needs of the individual learner and to provide immediate feedback make it possible for the teacher to ensure success in a situation where all too often there has been failure. The facility of some software (integrated learning systems, for example) to record progress is seen as a way of using ICT as a diagnostic tool, ensuring a close match between the tasks presented and the needs of the learner.

For teachers of learners with dyslexia, there is a desire to find a method of 'overlearning' spelling and reading patterns that will succeed where traditional classroom methods have failed. Often, the computer is seen as an answer and teachers will describe occasions where it has provided a successful method of practising specific skills. For the child with short-term memory or attention problems, the computer can be a regular prompter and incentive to stay on task.

Some integrated learning systems (ILS) provide spelling practice opportunities, but they were not designed with specific learning difficulties in mind. This means that the groupings of words in each session may be inappropriate and using them can even be counter-productive, if the intention was to increase the learner's confidence and self-esteem. Over the years, a large number of programs have been developed to reinforce particular teaching points. The question is, how suitable will they be for any individual learner? The criteria listed below provide a starting-point:

- **Can the speed of presentation and response be altered?**
  A program that flashes information onto the screen too quickly or requires a reaction beyond the capabilities of the learner will encourage guessing instead of a considered response; a program that moves too slowly will result in poor concentration. A long introduction is useful first time round, but becomes boring once you know it too well.

- **Is the display clear?**
  For learners who have problems with information processing, a cluttered screen with distracting colours and movement can hinder understanding.

- **Can the length of the game be altered?**
  A good game will allow the teacher to decide the number of goes or the success rate to be achieved for successful completion.

- **Can the sound level be altered?**
  A nasty noise that broadcasts the fact that you have made an error is not helpful for some learners.

- **Does the program save the settings?**
  It is a boon in a busy schedule if next time you come to the program, you can continue with the same options.

- **Does the program encourage the learner to work independently?**
  Is the task clear? Will the learner need to read on-screen instructions in order to tackle the required task? Are essential instructions spoken and/or can they be read by a screen reader if needed?

- **Can word lists be edited?**
  A good program will allow the teacher to enter word lists designed to support the learner's learning. Ease of editing and the ability to save lists of words rate highly in the choice of a flexible piece of software.

- **What happens when the learner makes a mistake?**
  There is nothing worse than getting caught in a loop where the software will not continue unless you get the answer right but provides no help if you get it wrong.

Having identified significant errors, activities can be created which use those target words. Programs such as Word Bar are useful for support and overlearning. Each word can be typed into a separate cell, with its definition or personal notes to jog the memory about how to spell it. Learners can scan through the grids to revise spellings or use them in written work.

Developing Tray and programs using cloze procedure such as Fun with Texts can be used to target particular spellings. The teacher types in a text containing a number of target words and saves the exercise. The file can then be opened and displayed on the screen as a series of blanks, waiting to be filled in. The teacher fills in some of the text, leaving only the key words blank. This is saved as a partly completed text. When the learner loads the text, only the target words need to be uncovered.

Alternatively you can set up a word list and the computer will generate a word search on the screen. This can be solved on screen or printed out to use away from the computer. The joy of programs such as GAMZ WordSearch or SPA's WordSquare Maker is that you can use any words the learner needs to focus on. You could put in science terms, vocabulary for geography or names of characters from play or novel. The words do not even have to be English as in the example above of regular –er verbs in French.

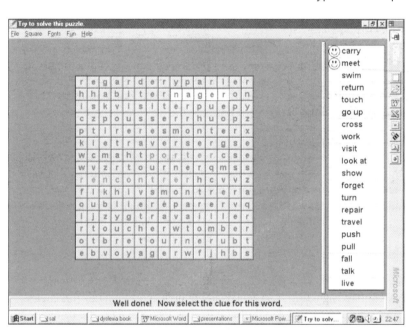

Wordsquare Player from SPA – hunting on screen for French verbs

spelling checkers

A spelling checker works by matching the individual words typed by the learner with the words in its dictionary. Any words that it does not recognise are displayed for the writer to check, including correct words that are not in its dictionary. In the majority of spell-checkers you have the choice of correcting the word, often with a list of suggestions to help you, or adding the word to the dictionary. A spell-checker will not differentiate between *see* and *sea* if both are in its dictionary.

All word-processing systems have built-in spell-checkers. These are getting better with each new version and often recognise common dyslexic errors too. The joy of spell-checkers is that they start with the words the learner wants or needs to use and not just a list out of context that practises a rule. On newer versions of Microsoft Word, incorrect words are underlined and clicking the right mouse button brings up spelling suggestions. They stop children from altering correct

1 Two pepal can play

2 You need a peise of paper and a pencle

3 You draw your one bord. The bord overlaps with to line across and too down

4 Someones norts and the other cosses, cosses are first that person go everywhere

A description of the game of noughts and crosses by an 11-year-old. The checker found and corrected 6 of the 10 mistakes.

1 Two **people** can play

2 You need a peise of paper and a **pencil**

3 You draw your one **board**. The **board** overlaps with to line across and too down

4 **Someone's** norts and the other cosses, cosses are first that person go **anywhere**

spellings – a common problem – and they offer instant support, which few teachers can match. In other words, they make learners begin to take responsibility for their own spelling.

some advantages of a word processor with a spell-checker

- It will check all the words you have written; this is useful for picking up words the learner is unsure of but might not ask about.

- It will confirm which words are already correct. One of the most interesting conclusions of Alan Crombie's research[1] was the usefulness of a spell-checker to 'protect what is correct'. Many pupils with dyslexia waste valuable time checking correct spellings unnecessarily, or worse still, altering them. The spell-checker focuses the learners' attention on the misspellings.

- It provides instant feedback and support which increase learner independence.

- Some provide a facility so the learner can hear the spelling as an additional check.

- You can add your own words to the dictionary. Words from specialist curriculum areas or personal vocabulary can be added to the dictionary to personalise it.

- The spelling can be checked while you are typing in. Many word processors with spell-checkers have a facility that bleeps if a misspelling is entered. It can be turned off, if it is found to be distracting.

- You can leave all spell checking until the end if it will interfere with the flow.

Some spell-checkers offer extra facilities such as a thesaurus where the user can check the meaning of words. Thesauruses help the student to extend their vocabulary and become more articulate but they can also provide a good spelling strategy for hard words: choose an easy synonym that you can spell, look it up, find the word you want and insert it in the document.

Really poor spellers benefit from 'AutoCorrect' which is found under the Tools menu on Word. This changes common mistakes to correct spellings when the user hits the space bar or full stop. Some people have achieved dramatic improvements by adding, with help, their most frequent 50 (or 100) common errors.

TextHelp is interesting because it combines many of the features dyslexic learners need in one package which can be used as an add-on to a standard word processor. It offers speech support so you can have text read back. It has a thesaurus button so you can highlight a word and have an alternative suggestion. You can set the spell-check options so it will check spellings as you type or at the end.

It will identify homophones as well as orthographical errors; it can also be set to find errors that are anagrams of the word you want and typical dyslexic phonetic errors. It also offers a prediction facility so as you type it suggests the

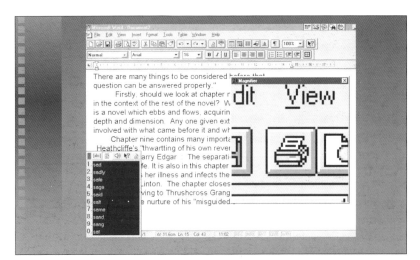

Using TextHelp with its prediction facility

words on screen. This has proved to be a very popular program although some users are finding that the little wizard who appears on screen when the speaking option is switched on is a real distraction.

Some people argue that the use of spell-checkers is akin to cheating and that pupils should be learning their spellings. There are two answers to this. Some

[1] See *Computers and Literacy Skills*, edited by Chris Singleton, BDA, 1991

children spend so much time on basic spelling that they accomplish little else and they still fail; these tools give them a little additional help when they need it. Secondly, many people learn to spell from using spell-checkers simply because they see their chosen words correctly spelt again and again instead of seeing several different botched efforts. There is an increasing body of evidence that if children write words incorrectly they will learn the misspellings and it becomes harder to teach them correct spellings. With a spell-checker they are seeing correctly spelt words and, because they are having the same words corrected again and again, they learn the new spelling. Some teachers also feel that having words corrected in context makes new spelling patterns fix in the learner's mind. Certainly there are many examples of learners who use a drill and practice spelling program very successfully and obtain a high score but under pressure they will revert to a previously learnt (wrong) spelling.

In addition to spell-checkers which are part of a word processor, there are also hand-held spell-checkers. Franklin's Elementary Spellmaster was designed to cope with spelling rather than typing errors, so tends to be more successful at identifying errors. Some learners use the computer spell-checker to identify the problem word and if too many or no solutions are provided, use the Spellmaster to help with identification.

some advantages of a hand-held spell-checker

- It can be used at any time. Learners can check the spelling of handwritten work such as labelling a diagram in science.
- Learners with neat handwriting and/or poor keyboard skills often prefer to handwrite their work and need access to a spell checker. Learners who get positive feedback from the look of their handwritten work are unlikely to want to lose that feeling of success and pride in their work by turning to the word processor, especially if the only print-out possible is one size, on an inferior printer. It depends on what a learner's perception of a successful writer is; if neatness is synonymous with success, then learners will often prefer a hand-held device to a word processor.
- Learners can use the spell-checker to practise their own spelling lists or have quick reference to a subject-specific list.
- Learners can check words where they know some of the letters.

grammar checkers

Grammar checkers claim to check:

- the spelling
- the use of words
- the punctuation
- the grammar
- the readability of a document.

As well as identifying 'errors', a grammar checker will usually be programmed to suggest improvements. For example, "John and me went fishing" will make the grammar checker display a specific message advising you to replace 'me' with 'I', while the over-use of passive verbs or very long sentences will show up as a general aspect of your writing style which may be worth changing. The National Literacy Framework states that primary school pupils should 'have a suitable technical vocabulary through which to understand and discuss their reading' and some schools are finding that the use of grammar checkers can help to provide this.

Careful planning for implementing the use of this kind of software is vital. Teachers will have to plan the introduction of the software to the learners as well as plan for how it is to be used. Learners need to be able to read the suggestions or they are just being given an extra burden to face. Checking spelling at the same time as

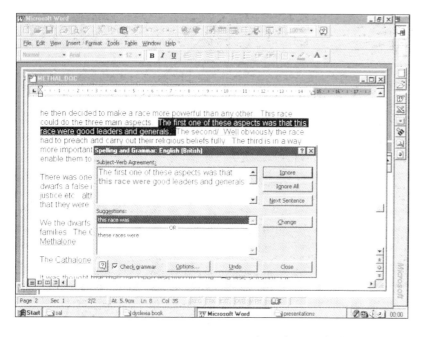

Using Word's spelling and grammar checker

grammar can be confusing for younger learners, so the advice is to check the spelling first before going to the grammar checker.

Older learners may be better able to cope with both checks happening at once, and thus see the proof-reading stage of writing in a more holistic way. However, experience with some older students shows that they can suffer from information overload, and they can get very frustrated by the need to disentangle useful advice from that which is irrelevant or inappropriate.

The major piece of advice, however, is that learners of all ages must have the confidence to be able to ignore any suggestion which appears on the screen. Some suggestions will be pure nonsense, springing from the limitations of the software; some will make learners pause for thought, ask questions, and try to understand why it has made the suggestion. However, when faced with corrections, learners must be able to say no and be ready to say why.

Finally, there is some evidence that, when they proof-read their writing in this way, learners discover and correct many of the things their teachers might have noticed for them. The one task that still seems to dominate teachers' reading of their learners' work is proof-reading. If grammar checkers and spell-checkers eradicate the most obvious errors, could we be at last on the verge of a revolution in the way teachers read learners' writing? Will teachers at last feel able to devote as much attention to the content of what they read?

new technologies – benefit or burden?

The World Wide Web (WWW) offers access to exciting, motivating and curriculum-focused materials. The content ranges from highly focused learning materials and revision aids through to rich, beautifully produced resources with full colour multimedia from organisations and media producers across the world but it also offers challenges for learners with dyslexia and literacy problems.

Teachers can benefit from the National Grid for Learning (NGfL) (http://www.ngfl.gov.uk/) which provides a means for schools to connect to the Internet, training opportunities for teachers in the use of ICT, and a dedicated Web area which brings together appropriate UK resources.

If teachers want to keep abreast of the latest thinking on dyslexia they should look at the Schools area of the NGfL, the DfEE SEN information and Becta's Web site (http://www.becta.org.uk). These provide information and, more importantly, links to sources of expertise and resources on dyslexia. They might like to join the Dyslexia mailing list, which enables teachers to share concerns and discuss issues of particular concern to dyslexics through the use of e-mail. The list acts as both a discussion forum for dyslexics and for the research community (in the UK), as a source of information about and access to, dyslexics. It gives particular attention to computer tools that dyslexics find to be useful.

Messages on the Dyslexia mailing list

But what about dyslexic learners? Here the picture is not quite so clear. There are undoubted benefits in that they can access on-line reference materials. This can be easier than wading through volumes of an encyclopaedia or indexes and content listings. However, the Web is not as tolerant of spelling mistakes as many of the CD-ROM encyclopaedias. If you type in a search term which it doesn't recognise, such as *eejipt* instead of Egypt, the search engine will usually not come up with any results. In addition, many pupils are overwhelmed by the sheer volume of irrelevant information which is thrown up and do not necessarily have the skimming and scanning skills to decide what to reject.

Navigating content on the Web can involve typing in long location addresses (URLs), such as http://www.xxxxxx, storing these locations as 'bookmarks' so that you can return to that Web site and also navigating using highlighted links and icons through a Web site. All of these tasks can present challenges for learners. The

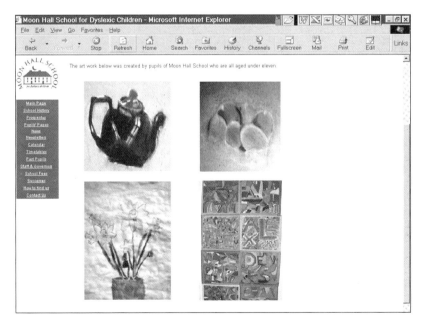

A site featuring the work of dyslexic pupils
Reproduced by permission of Moon Hall School

addresses need to be typed exactly and are case sensitive, book marks can grow in number and to be useful need organising in logical folders or groupings. It is also easy to feel lost after following a series of links.

Technology can be used to support learners in these tasks. The type and amount of support will depend of the learner's particular needs. Screen readers (which use synthetic speech to read back any text on the computer screen) and talking Web

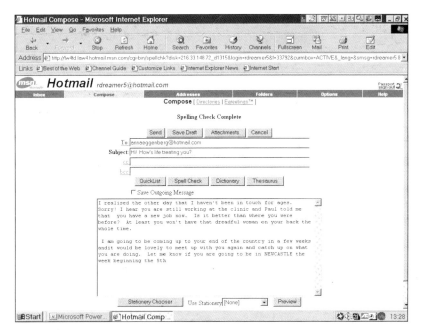

browsers can provide audio cues. This can work particularly well when text versions of the Web page are available. A good example of this can be seen on the BBC Web site where they have developed software (called BETSIE) which turns each page into a screen-readable format. Some dyslexic learners have found that the Web has played to their strengths and there are some stunning sites featuring students' work.

On-screen grids can be designed to provide a meaningful visual which when clicked on opens the appropriate site. For example, a Clicker Grid with an image of a dinosaur can have a Web address linked to it so that when selected, the address is sent to the Web browser and that site is loaded. The Web browser itself can be set up to provide the background, text and links in the colours that the learner prefers and also the font style and size of choice.

Some e-mail software also has spell-checker features

Alison finds the Internet a pain. She has always had problems with phone numbers and finds it hard to get the right number of digits in the right order. "Conventional addresses have a structure: the house number, the road, the district, the town etc. In fact, Internet addresses also have a structure but if this has not been explained, it is meaningless and they are eminently forgettable."

She explains, "The new etiquette leads to overload. When you ring a voice mail and get a messaging service, people don't say "You can reach me at..." and then reel off a whole address but they are starting to do that with e-mail addresses." Alison admits that she usually only corresponds with people if they have contacted her first. Then she can just click on Reply.

Getting information is not easy either. The Internet is a pathway with branches off so it is easy to get lost quite quickly. Alison finds the Internet is not too bad for browsing, but hunting and gathering information is difficult because of short-term memory problems. "Bookmarking is only a partial solution; you need to remember what a particular bookmark means and where a train of thought is going." She would like to see more sophisticated tracking tools of the kind which are commonplace in multimedia applications. Ideally, you would click and see a storyboard or pictorial representation of all the screens you have called up and be able to edit them.

E-mail

E-mail can provide similar benefits and challenges. "It beats writing a letter!" is how Michelle, a 15-year-old pupil described it. She likes the fact that it is quick. You are not expected to write much at any one time whereas letters less than six lines long are somehow not seen as a proper piece of work. You can write off-line with all the tools mentioned in this book: spell-checkers, grammar checkers, predictive packages or voice input, and get the text right before going on-line to send it. On the other hand, it is also a medium where 'typing errors' are tolerated. We would not expect to receive a letter with three or four errors in it but we are far less critical of the spelling in e-mails and do not necessarily make judgements about the sender.

However, there are particular skills and conventions needed when writing e-mail addresses, organising address books and creating e-mails. You can find ideas and advice on this in Becta's *From Chalkboard to Internet* or on Becta's Web site (http://www.becta.org.uk).

the Literacy Hour

The National Literacy Strategy Framework for Teaching lays down what children are expected to achieve. Some of these are of particular interest to those who work with dyslexic learners. For example:

> …be able to orchestrate a full range of reading cues (phonic, graphic, syntactic, contextual) to monitor their reading and correct their own mistakes.

This is a crucial area for dyslexic learners as they are now being taught these skills in a very obvious and direct way whereas in the past they might have been expected to infer them from some of the classroom activities.

> …have fluent and legible handwriting.

Many dyslexics will never achieve this and may have to use word processing in order to make their work legible.

> …have an interest in words, their meanings and a growing vocabulary.

This is usually not a problem as many dyslexic learners have an exceptionally wide ranging adventurous spoken vocabulary and now will receive recognition for this.

> …plan, draft, revise and edit their own writing.

Word substitution exercise from Wellington Square

Teachers have found for years that this is the way forward to improve literacy for all pupils but that with the aid of a word processor we have been able to make dyslexic learners more independent and that they have started to proof-read and be more critical of their work.

The Literacy Hour structures the time on a daily basis to ensure that every pupil is receiving the same sort of input. In the future we will know what pupils have been taught, even if there is still a question mark over what some of them have learned!

Children have 15 minutes of whole class reading and writing and 15 minutes of word level work, 20 minutes of guided group and independent work and 10 minutes for the plenary session. In some ways the final plenary session is the most useful for dyslexic learners because this gives them a chance to recap and verbalise what they have been doing and this seems to help them fix things in their mind. The fact that the Literacy Hour is very structured and they will be doing the same types of activities on a regular basis provides a sound structure for the unconfident learner. Moreover, the guidance states that pupils with identified special needs may require additional support but

> should not automatically be put into the lowest ability groups. Many pupils who have specific difficulties with literacy skills may have the same, or even better, conceptual understanding as the pupils in the highest ability group.

Technology has an important role to play in the Literacy Hour. Some software provides differentiation to cater for pupils at all ability levels, giving them extra support when and where it is needed and an extended range of activities.

Many teachers report that children concentrate for longer when using the computer and are also less easily distracted by other pupils. Software such as abc-CD from Sherston helps young children to learn the sounds and shapes of the alphabet while Claude and Maud offers handwriting practice.

There is a host of materials for onset and rhyme from companies such as Crick and Sherston and a proliferation of CD-ROMs designed to support Literacy Hour teaching. Wellington Square, based on the Nelson reading scheme, contains word classification and rhyming activities, phonics exercises, initial and final blends, and vowel sounds.

Stories are still important in the Literacy Hour. Book Spinner is a clever program from Widgit Software that helps pupils and teachers to produce books. It does all the pagination for you, and once you choose layout and font and it will load in the relevant character sets. There is a range of graphics on the CD, and it will make little books (about the size of the Mr Men series) or a Big Book for the Literacy Hour.

Talking stories widely used at present include Rainbow Stories from Resource, Oxford Reading Tree Talking Stories and Sherston's Naughty Stories. These have been the subject of research to see if they offer more than just entertainment (see http://www.sherston.com/literacy/). Jane Medwell, University of Warwick, found that the use of talking books:

- increases children's word reading accuracy, both in the context of the story and out of context
- improves children's understanding of the stories and supports children's reading by offering them access to the meaning of the stories and the way sentences work
- is more effective for boys who seemed to show greater increases in word accuracy than girls when using the talking stories. Considering that most struggling readers are boys, this is a valuable resource.

Technology can also support the teacher because there is a range of activities and materials on-line and for the first time there is probably as much material available electronically to support the work in the classroom as there is in printed form. The NGfL Web site and in particular the Virtual Teacher Centre (VTC) provide links to sources of advice and information on literacy and how ICT can support learners with a wide range of needs. The Literacy Time site on the VTC (http://vtc.ngfl.gov.uk/ resource/literacy/index.html) provides examples of ways schools are ensuring learners with special needs are included and the Classroom Resources section also gives examples of practical activities, reviews of software and examples of good practice. You might try typing in 'literacy hour' on a search engine to get a range of sites.

dyslexia and mathematics

[handwritten note: younger (c) use app. bypass using strategies]

Some children have problems with reversing numbers and sequences of numbers, due to perceptual or sequencing difficulties related to their cognitive weaknesses. For younger children, this may be a developmental phase, for which the young learner can develop bypass strategies. Such children usually understand the maths and some are good mathematicians, once they can read sufficiently to complete their work. Others have a much more deep-seated problem (dyscalculia), which requires specialist structured teaching.

[handwritten note: Mental starter – Long T memory, not asked to write on paper.]

The Numeracy Strategy promotes the use of mental strategies and the whole class will be spending 5-10 minutes each day sharpening and developing mental and oral maths skills. Some children with dyslexia excel in this area if they do not have major difficulties with long-term memory. Many like the fact that they are not called upon to put something down on paper with all the attendant problems that poses.

There are, however, some prescribed and linear approaches to calculations that may disadvantage the pupil with dyslexia who may benefit from alternative strategies. Teachers will need to be aware that when applying the National Numeracy Strategy, they may have to adapt some of their methods if they are not to leave dyslexic pupils behind. *[handwritten note: What methods?]*

Where learners have difficulty reading maths textbooks, they will not be able to do maths independently, however great their mathematical ability. Some schools get volunteers to tape the textbook, so the poor reader can listen to the tape while reading the question. Some learners benefit from working through a remedial programme which includes ICT. Tables can be a particular problem. Software includes Number Shark and the new What do you do when you can't learn the Times Tables which presents information visually and orally. It also suggests some strategies and shows how to make good use of prior knowledge. However, for others the struggle is not worth the effort and it is better to teach them strategies such as how to use a calculator and a number square for tables.

Lindsey has mild cerebral palsy and related dyslexic and dyscalculic specific learning difficulties. At 13 years, she still had spatial awareness problems, especially when asked to manipulate objects in space. Tangrams were a particular nightmare and cutting up cards to make shapes fit was very frustrating. Using the tangram screens on My World, she could drag shapes around the screen easily, until she found a good fit. The first two took her twenty minutes to solve, but then she realised what was involved and romped through the rest of the screens.

Some of the early concept work in maths involves much drawing, colouring, cutting and sticking before the child moves to the 'What if…?' stage. For many children this provides good concrete experience of handling shapes but for others, this practical work can be such an obstacle that they rarely reach the mathematical part. Some practical work is essential, but using suitable My World screens reduces the frustration and enables pupils to move on to the thinking element. If the exercise involves using blocks, cubes, rods or shapes, pupils will benefit from manipulating the real objects, and My World screens can be used for recording and then printing out the work. *Seeing* and *doing* are the watchwords for teaching mathematics to dyslexic learners. It is essential to minimise verbal explanations. If the learner is given a sequence of instructions before carrying out a task, he or she is doubly handicapped. Firstly, short-term memory may be at fault so one instruction may be omitted and secondly, where sequencing is a problem, he or she may get the order wrong. Learners must be encouraged to see how numbers fit into patterns, rather than relying on memorising facts.

Dyslexics may find the following difficult:

- counting
- visualising numbers
- directional problems
- notation and orientation of numbers
- sequencing – does 3.5 come before 4.2?
- place value
- symbols
- language of maths

[handwritten note: Probs for dyscalculia]

- number bonds
- remembering times tables
- recognising and naming shapes
- patterns.

There are no quick solutions to these problems and we need to acknowledge that they exist and try to find ways of helping the student to overcome them. Above all, we need to learn from the learner. What can they do successfully? How did they learn to do that? Can the strategies they used be applied to a new topic or set of skills? The teacher's role is to provide support and to focus on strategies which can be used independently by the learner.

Dr Steve Chinn, principal of Mark College in Somerset, has produced a number of books describing strategies for developing good maths skills with dyslexic learners. He recommends a variety of approaches including using concrete materials to develop concepts. We do this a lot with younger children, of course, but expect them to move on to more abstract representations. If a child needs to count on his or her fingers or use a ruler as a number line long after the rest of the class have moved on, then so be it. The maths and the child's confidence are more important than other issues. Software can also provide a good staging post between concrete and abstract. Often the screens have things to be counted or moved around which are not quite as concrete as rods, cubes and sweets but can give reinforcement to those who are not quite sure of their number facts. Make sure that whatever software you use, the screens are uncluttered. Many modern maths books are designed to be visually appealing and while this is laudatory, it has led designers into creating pages which may have irrelevant graphics and a host of stylistic devices which are very tricky to read.

Teaching styles may have to change. Traditionally, staff worked on a topic such as fractions for a block of time and then moved on to another topic where they did a substantial amount of work. The problem with using this method with dyslexic learners is that they will forget much of it if there is a long gap before they revisit the topic. A better approach is to have lots of short blocks of work interspersed with revision and extension of previously learnt material. Again, computer programs can provide reinforcement of topics. The language of maths can also be a real handicap. There are lots of different ways of expressing the same concepts. Pupils need to be taught the language of maths and it should not be assumed that they will pick it up.

As with spell-checkers there is a school of thought which says that using calculators is cheating: people should not rely on the technology but should spend time learning tables and number bonds. There is little agreement on how this learning should happen since many of the tried and trusted methods have been used and have proved unsuccessful before the learner has been identified as having special needs. What is clear is that if pupils are going to use calculators effectively then they need to develop some estimating skills and sufficient awareness of number so they will reject ludicrous answers.

Many learners with dyslexia work very slowly and may fail to spot patterns because there is such a long interval between one worked example and another. Where children take an entire lesson to do six calculations and get two of them wrong, there is no possibility that these children could discover any pattern. The Interactive Calculator from Inclusive Technology combines clear visual presentation, auditory feedback and physical manipulation to help dyslexic learners. Unlike other calculators, this one comes with a 'guess' button to encourage estimation. It is also possible to turn off some of the features so that they can be introduced step by step as part of a managed learning programme.

Spreadsheets can also be a good way of encouraging pupils to have a go and experiment more confidently with numbers. Many students can perform the calculations necessary to solve a problem, but have difficulties recording their work. Setting up a spreadsheet can encourage good habits in the layout of problems, which may transfer to work with pen and paper. The student can see a problem set out before them, and is therefore less likely to get lost in the process of calculation.

apparatus

What's diff bet Concrete + Abstract?

interactive whiteboard resources

12 divided by 4 may be expressed as 4 divided into 12; 12 ÷ 4; 12/4 ; 12 shared between 4. They all mean the same thing but learners may not realise this.

Subtraction may be expressed as less, minus and take away. 12 take away 7 is the same as take 7 from 12, but which number is taken from which? How should it be written?

Teaching Styles

Nisha and Suran were using a calculator to learn about multiplying and dividing by 10. During the lesson they operated on more than twenty decimal numbers. They made tables in their books showing the starting numbers and the answers.

3.15	31.5	.315
56	560	5.6
112.7	1127	11.27
0.005	0.05	0.0005

When they had discovered the rules, they predicted the answers for a few more numbers and used the calculator as a check. Then they added extra columns to their table and proceeded with their investigation, exploring multiplication and division by 100, 1000 and other powers of 10.

Spreadsheets.

dyslexia and modern foreign languages

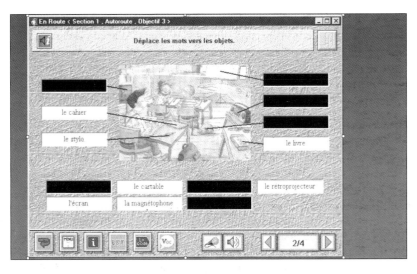

En Route from Granada Learning

The problem with dyslexia is, of course, that it affects learning throughout the curriculum. Problems in the early years with reading and writing tasks become problems in maths, history, geography, science, foreign languages – the whole curriculum – by the time the learner arrives at secondary school. Many of these problems can be alleviated by the strategies mentioned earlier, but there is a particular challenge in subjects such as modern foreign languages.

Some people believe that pupils should not start on a second language until they are proficient in their first. While bilingual children throughout the world develop their skills in two or more languages in tandem, parents and teachers worry that the dyslexic child will not cope with the additional stress of a new language with different spellings, sounds and written forms. They might fail yet again or muddle the two languages and lose the ground they have gained with English spelling.

In fact, many dyslexic learners capitalise on their good oral skills, their ability to learn and use vocabulary and their communication skills. When they are learning a new language, they are usually starting from scratch, on a par with most other learners and the strategies which work for the first language tend to work for others. This may be because of greater maturity or because the learners have discovered certain learning styles which work for them.

The case of Martin, a 15-year-old learning French, highlights both the problems dyslexics may encounter and some strategies for overcoming them.

Martin was a very poor reader till age of 11 and had considerable problems with phonics, syllabification and orthographical memory. In English he had overcome these problems through a variety of strategies, including looking for little words in the big word and lots of work on word patterns. He used a spellchecker which gave him instant feedback on his spelling mistakes and helped him to identify frequently repeated errors.

Je suis... Is that *I have*? After four years of French classes at school with a teacher who was a native speaker and several trips to France, Martin reached Year 11 with virtually no knowledge of French. The communicative method had given him quite a lot of passive language but also left him frustrated: "I can't say even the simplest thing!".

However, he had a reasonable accent, a willingness to have a go and was less inhibited than most 15-year-olds. He had a belief that it could be possible to master the subject but was aware that time was running out and he would have to do something.

His teacher wanted to bring together words, pictures and sounds to create a multi-sensory approach. Since every child learns differently, by using as many input methods as possible, we are likely to find ways which work for the child. At the same time it was important to find lots of really good and interesting ways of revisiting the same vocabulary or structures again and again without boring the learner. Martin needed to:

- see the whole picture
- work on a set of rules and apply them to make new structures
- have some physical activity touching and moving words as well as copying them
- reflect on and verbalise what he was doing
- engage in some kind of creative activity to use language actively.

Multimedia CD-ROMs can offer good support in this area. Many are topic based and bring together the vocabulary and common phrases needed for particular situations.

With a CD-ROM, we see a picture, click, listen and compare. Unlike real life, we are in total control and can go back again and again to revisit particular words. There are limits to the number of times we can ask a French host "*Qu'est ce que c'est?*" or "*Qu'est ce que ça veut dire?*" but the patient computer tells us again and again with the same words, accent and intonation.

At the same time, Martin needed to reinforce some of the Year 7 work. They found that Clicker can be used to develop and give support in a second language in exactly the same way as it does in English. There are some sample French grids in Clicker 3 which can be used to support writing. For example, in the *j'ai* grid, a student can build simple sentences.

Clicker French

The pictures offered a valuable support. The use of real speech meant that Martin could listen to a good model of correct accent and intonation and start to link sound and spelling, just as he had done in English.

The Food and I Go grids make different use of sampled speech. In both cases the grid fills the screen and the emphasis is on listening rather than writing. In the first example, click on each food item with the left mouse button to hear a word and focus on the sound. Then as you click with the right button, you hear the French word in a sentence.

Martin found Clicker 3 French grids very helpful. Hearing the word in context helped him to remember. His teacher chose verbs as a starting point for rules. Martin knew lots of nouns: *La banque, l'addition, thé* and some common phrases such as *J'ai besoin de...* and *Quelle heure est-il?* but had no recognition that *ai* was from *avoir* and that it would be possible to say '*Nous avons besoin de...*' because he had never heard this structure. They started with regular –er verbs with the objectives of being able to use them in the present tense, the future and the simple past. The advantage of this approach was that it would give him lots of vocabulary all at once as there are so many regular –er verbs.

Martin and his teacher used various programs to devise ways of overlearning the verbs. The word processor was invaluable because it meant they could record a neat copy. Like many pupils, Martin was prone to losing things so it was a good idea to have a French folder which had masters of the notes. Another advantage was that the words were legible. It is hard to pronounce foreign words if you are not sure if the letter is an 'n' or an 'r' – *oublier* or *onblier*?

They spent a lot of time pairing English and French words. Here Excel was useful. Column A had French words, column B contained English equivalents:

manger	eat
parler	speak
fumer	smoke
gagner	earn
chercher	look for
détester	hate
inviter	invite
jouer	play
aider	help
louer	rent/hire

By selecting column B and clicking on 'Sort ascending' which put the English words in alphabetical order, they devised a new list which could be printed out for matching activities.

manger	look for
parler	earn
fumer	eat
gagner	hate
chercher	help
détester	invite
inviter	play

jouer	rent /hire
aider	smoke
louer	speak

They had the first version saved as a reference copy so Martin could check his answers for himself and be more actively engaged in the learning process. They also printed out the table and cut it up to make flash-cards for daily revision.

To start with Martin found it hard to recognise and pronounce the French words but day by day his confidence improved and soon he became fluent at finding the French words and being able to use them in sentences, working from a model. He was delighted that he could begin to create new structures he had never seen or heard before.

The technology motivated him because it gave him access to neatly written text which he could decipher, lots of good models of speech for listening practice and a great variety of activities which stopped him from getting bored. Martin is now beginning to explore the Web and looking at some of the French sites. Although he is not able to understand much of the text, he is delighted when he finds phrases he recognises or can get the gist of an item in French.

Crosswords and word hunts were mentioned earlier in conjunction with spelling. Because they are frameworks programs, they can just as easily support French words. They are a good way of creating relevant, age-appropriate materials. Using SPA software, exercises can be very easily made easy to tailor to specific vocabulary, English or French.

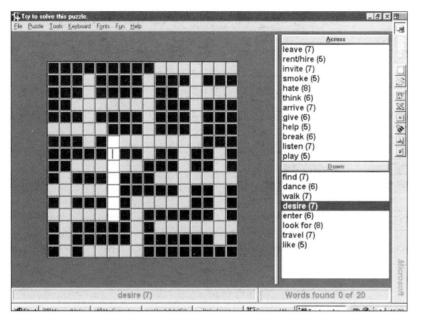

Crossword software can contain foreign vocabulary just as easily as English

appendix a: choosing software

Listed below are a number of software titles and peripherals which can be used to help develop particular skills. Please note that inclusion in the list does not imply recommendation by Becta, or exclusion imply the reverse.

Key:

Ac	Acorn
Mac	Apple Macintosh
PC	IBM compatible
EY	Early Years

software to support planning

Title	Publisher	Platform	Age
I Can Write	Resource	Ac/PC	KS1/2/3
A supportive program for generating word, phrase and topic banks to support unconfident writers. Also helpful for helping disorganised writers to plan their ideas.			
IDONS	IDONS	PC	KS3/4/Adult
Planning software for preparing information for essays, reports and revision.			
Inspiration	iANSYST	PC/Mac	KS2-Adult
Planning software for computerised mindmaps for organising ideas for essays, reports and revision.			
SMOG	Inclusive Technology	PC	Adult
A utility for teachers to use to check the reading level of text. Especially useful for worksheets that were written on the computer.			
Student Report Writer	Ablac	PC/Mac	KS4
Guides the student through the logical stages of preparing written work and gives ideas for improving writing styles for different purposes.			
Thinksheet	Fisher-Marriott	Ac/PC	KS2/3/4/Adult
The equivalent of an electronic flip chart, where ideas can be typed rapidly into boxes and later dragged and dropped through the appropriate keyhole to make an essay or report. A preliminary list of text can be viewed, revised and then dropped into a word processor for expansion into a full essay. For the really disorganised, the teacher can prepare the frame for an essay, into which the pupil can add details.			
Wordbar	Crick	PC	KS3/4/Adult
A compact on-screen word facility that helps with spelling and organising phrases for producing reports and essays. It can be used with a full desktop or CE Windows word processors.			
Wordswork	iANSYST	PC	KS4/Adult
A multimedia, interactive tool for students with dyslexia to come to terms with their problems and find ways of remediating them. Some KS4 students could find it helpful with guidance from the SENCO.			

software to support identification of dyslexia and SpLD

Title	Publisher	Platform	Age
ABC CD	Sherston	Ac/Mac/PC	KS1/2
	Uses digitised speech, animation and morphing graphics in 3 games that deal with visual and aural letter discrimination and recognition.		
LASS	Lucid	PC	KS3/4
	An identification program of computer games for teachers to use to discover the learning style, strengths and weaknesses of secondary pupils who are having problems with literacy and numeracy.		
CoPS	Lucid	Ac/Mac/PC	EY/KS1
	A psychometric assessment system to enable teachers and other appropriately trained and qualified people to identify children's cognitive strengths and weaknesses.		
ScanIT	Maia Learning Systems	PC	KS2/3/4
	Designed to improve reading speed and accuracy. Back-up logging system records progress and increases speed as the pupil progresses. Words, phrases and sentences can be provided in the files, with increasingly subtle distracters, which can be useful for identifying the type of reading errors being made. Useful for developing skills to stay on task.		
Study Scan	Interactive Services Ltd	PC	Adult
	A screening program for colleges to establish where students have dyslexic learning difficulties.		
Wordswork	iANSYST	PC	KS4/Adult
	A multimedia, interactive tool for students with dyslexia to come to terms with their problems and find ways of remediating them. Some KS4 students could find it helpful with guidance from the SENCO.		

software to support reading

Title	Publisher	Platform	Age
All my words	Crick	PC	EY/KS1/2
	A wide range of reading, writing and spelling activities, with words, pictures and sounds. Activities can be reading differentiated to also provide progression. Large number of ready-made activities, but can be easily customised.		
Bailey's Book House	Iona	PC/Mac	EY/KS1
	A multi-sensory reading experience with music, words and sentences that speak. There is an Explore and Discover mode for learning and Question and Answer for consolidation. Activities include letter sounds and names, rhyming, meanings of words.		
Cambridge Reading My Pet	Sherston	Ac/Mac/PC	KS1
	Six talking books from the Beginning to Read phase of the CUP reading scheme. Talking text and some animation.		

Title	Publisher	Platform	Age
Catch Up	Oxford Brookes	PC	KS2

In 5 separate video-type games the children match, sort, look/cover/write, use onset and rime with a graded set of high frequency words. Very attractive software designed to be part of the Catchup scheme to raise the literacy skills of Year 3 children at level 1 in KS1 SATs. Most effective if used as part of the whole scheme, but is still useful if the word lists coincide with what the children are being taught by other means.

Title	Publisher	Platform	Age
Children's Dictionary	Dorling Kindersley	PC/Mac	KS2/3

An interactive dictionary of 37,000 words with pictures, sounds and animation as well as some word games. Very supportive and encouraging for developing dictionary skills for poor readers/spellers.

Title	Publisher	Platform	Age
Clicker Plus Talking Books	Crick	Ac/Mac/PC	KS1/2

Three ready-made stories, with real speech, and an outline file for making your own talking stories on Clicker Plus.

Title	Publisher	Platform	Age
Electronic Library	Carron	PC	KS2/3/4

A collection of 200 talking stories designed to promote reading and spelling skills, especially for those with difficulties. The pupil reads the books and does the spelling routines alone, which is made possible by the text speaking on request. Story pages can be printed out to read away from the computer for reinforcement and the spellings should be written in a paper file, to provide multi-sensory skill acquisition.

Title	Publisher	Platform	Age
First Keys to Literacy	Widgit	PC	KS1/2/3

Designed for teaching young children the keyboard layout, this program can be used additionally to develop reading and spelling skills in a structured way. There are many sample files and graphics to use straight away, and it is easy to tweak existing files or make your own. KS2 and even KS3 children enjoy using it if the files are adapted to their vocabulary needs.

Title	Publisher	Platform	Age
Flash Cards	Eurotalk	PC/Mac	KS1/2

These are really designed to learn another language, so there are options to explore the words, play games and record your own efforts. Games include: Find the card; Match the pairs; Beat the Clock which could be useful activities for the dyslexic child to use at home for visual discrimination memory training and improving speed. Foreign language versions provide extra support for learning new vocabulary, especially at home.

Title	Publisher	Platform	Age
Fun With Texts	Camsort	Ac/Mac/PC	KS3/4/Adult

Contains a Concordance program, which replaces the old word-frequency program. Language modules are available to enable the user to set up the program so that on-screen instructions are in the target language.

Title	Publisher	Platform	Age
Fuzzbuzz	Semerc	PC/Mac	KS1/2
Interactive activities to support the Fuzzbuzz reading scheme.			
Granny's Garden	4Mation	Ac/PC	KS1/2
One of the very first educational adventure games, it has now been developed for use on multimedia machines and is still popular for combining reading and thinking skills with a new generation of learners.			
Jolly Post Office	Dorling Kindersley	PC/Mac	EY/KS1
Sorting, sequencing, designing stamps, sending postcards can be practised in a Post Office environment.			
Keystone	Words Worldwide	PC	KS3/4/Adult
A utility to run with Dragon Dictate to facilitate editing, as it provides computer-speak feedback of the text entered by voice recognition, which may have put in correctly spelt, but wrong words.			
Learn English/ French/Spanish/ German/ Italian/ Russian/Japanese	Camsoft	PC/Mac	KS2-Adult
A series of interactive CD-ROMs intended to develop fluency in everyday use of foreign languages. The foreign ones could be useful to use at home or in homework clubs for practising scenarios that have been learned in MFL lessons; the English disc is another way of reinforcing word recognition and spelling.			
Living Books 1	Broderbund	PC/Mac	EY/KS1
Dr Seuss's Cat in the Hat; *Green Eggs and Ham*; *Dr Seuss's ABC*; *Just Grandma and Me*; *Tortoise and the Hare*. Interactive talking books to encourage young readers.			
Living Books 2	Broderbund	PC/Mac	KS1/2
Arthur's Birthday; *Arthur's Teacher Trouble*; *Harry and the Haunted House*; *Little Monster at School*; *Darby the Dragon*. Interactive talking books to encourage young readers, but suitable for older unwilling readers.			
Look Hear	Sherston	Ac	KS1
Body/Dinosaurs/Homes/Land transport/Pet. Talking reference books for infants, but dyslexic children even at KS2 enjoy using them to find things out for themselves.			
Making Sense With Words	Inclusive Technology	PC	KS2/3
Multi-sensory activities with groups of words to encourage reading, comprehension, spelling and learning about parts of speech.			

Title	Publisher	Platform	Age
Matti Mole's Summer holiday	Sherston	Ac/Mac/PC	KS2

Designed for general use for younger KS2 pupils for language development, but there is so much speech support, it would be useful even into lower secondary school for pupils with reading problems, to have the experience of doing English work more independently.

Title	Publisher	Platform	Age
My First Incredible Amazing Talking Dictionary	Dorling Kindersley	PC/Mac	KS1/2

Interactive multimedia dictionary of 1000 words to help young readers learn how to use a dictionary.

Title	Publisher	Platform	Age
My World: Fun Phonics	Semerc	Ac/PC	KS1/2

Screens to provide extension activities for developing literacy skills.

Title	Publisher	Platform	Age
Naughty Stories	Sherston	Ac/Mac/PC	EY/KS1

A set of talking reading books for young children. They can follow the story on the screen even before they can read and there are paper copies of the book as well. Animations on the screen are motivating and a background record is kept of any words the child asks for help with.

Title	Publisher	Platform	Age
New Reading Disc	Cambridge Training and Development	PC	Adult

An interactive multimedia tool for supporting the development of literacy skills in adults. Also useful for writing, and developing study and life skills at KS4.

Title	Publisher	Platform	Age
Oxford Reading Tree	Sherston	Ac/Mac/PC	KS1

Talking books with text highlighted as it is spoken and animations of the pictures to support the Oxford Reading Tree books.

Title	Publisher	Platform	Age
Rainbow Stories	Resource	PC	KS2/3

A selection of talking books with 6 stories and 3 games retelling old favourites and read by a wide range of voices.

Title	Publisher	Platform	Age
Reading Schemes	NASEN	PC	KS1/2/3

An interactive summary of the NASEN Guide to Reading Schemes. All the advantages of the book, with the added database search facility and sample pages of some books.

Title	Publisher	Platform	Age
Ridiculous Rhymes	Sherston	Ac/PC	KS2/3

Talking humorous rhymes with animations, which are fun but also provide reinforcement of rhyming skills.

Title	Publisher	Platform	Age
Rusty Dreamer	Sherston	Ac/Mac/PC	KS2/3

A talking reading book for older readers. It can be read at 3 levels, with increasing amounts of text.

Title	Publisher	Platform	Age
Symbols to Sentences	Widgit	Ac	KS1/2/3
Runs talking rebus supported reading and spelling activities on the Acorn that were made on Writing with Symbols.			
TextHELP!	TextHELP Systems	PC	KS3/4/Adult
A utility to run in Windows to provide audio support for text in other programs. Words, phrases, sentences or paragraphs can be selected to be spoken. Also has text prediction and abbreviation facilities.			
Ultimate Speed Reader	Ablac	PC/Mac	KS2/3/4/Adult
There is no speech support, but this program measures your speed of reading and tests you for accuracy of comprehension.			
Units of Sound	Dyslexia Institute	PC	KS2/3/4/Adult
A reading development programme which can also be used for skill building in spelling and writing.			
Wellington Square	Semerc	PC/Mac	KS2/3
An extensive range of interactive, multimedia activities to support and extend the reading scheme, which includes talking versions of the books.			
Writing with Symbols	Widgit	Ac/PC	KS2/3/4/Adult
A rebus word processor, which can be used to make talking rebus supported materials on the (Acorn) computer and printed out as rebus supported text.			

software to support spelling

Title	Publisher	Platform	Age
ABC CD	Sherston	Ac/Mac/PC	KS1/2
Uses digitised speech, animation and morphing graphics in 3 games that deal with visual and aural letter discrimination and recognition.			
AcceleRead and AcceleWrite	iANSYST, REM	Book	KS2/3/4
A book providing materials and explaining how to use a talking word processor.			
All My Words	Crick	PC	EY/ KS1/2
A wide range of reading, writing and spelling activities, with words, pictures and sounds. Activities can be reading differentiated to also provide progression. Large number of ready-made activities, but can be easily customised.			
Children's Dictionary	Dorling Kindersley	PC/Mac	KS2/3
An interactive dictionary of 37,000 words with pictures, sounds and animation as well as some word games. Very supportive and encouraging for developing dictionary skills for poor reader/spellers.			

Title	Publisher	Platform	Age
Cloze	Semerc	PC	KS2/3/4
A utility for creating screen cloze exercises.			
Co:Writer	Don Johnston	PC/Mac	KS2/3/4/Adult
An on-screen, talking support for spelling prediction that can be used with Write Outloud or other word processors.			
Crosswords	SPA	PC	KS1/2/3/4
Enables the user to make two types of puzzles, a normal crossword with clues given for across and down, or a grid puzzle with words listed according to their length.			
Crossword Callup	REM	Ac/PC	KS2/3/4/Adult
A crossword-generating program that can be useful for extra practice of new curriculum words.			
Dyspell	Sally Systems	Ac/PC	KS2/3/4
A multi-sensory spelling training program, where the child works at a level where success is guaranteed and rewarded with regular certificates as progress is made.			
Eye for Spelling	LDA	Ac/Mac/PC	KS1/2
Structured spelling program, which also provides a visual prompt of how to write the word in script. Comes with many sample files, which can be re-organised or amended with extra words.			
First Keys to Literacy	Widgit	PC	KS1/2/3
Designed for teaching young children the keyboard layout, this program can be used additionally to develop reading and spelling skills in a structured way. There are many sample files and graphics to use straight away, and it is easy to tweak existing files or make your own. KS2 and even KS3 children enjoy using it if the files are adapted to their vocabulary needs.			
Fleet Street Phantom	Sherston	Ac/PC	KS2/3
Adventure with problem solving related to punctuation and spelling.			
Franklin Spellmasters	Franklin	Peripheral	KS1/2/3/Adult
A range of sturdy, stand-alone spelling aids to support different levels of spelling problems. The Elementary Spellmaster has been a useful support for many years but has gone out of production. The Language master has speech support, is slower, but some dyslexic users like it. Elementary Spellmaster (with OUP Children's Dictionary); SPQ106 Spellmaster; DMQ210 Pocket Dictionary; TPQ106 Wordmaster; DMQ440 Dictionary; Language Master.			
GAMZ2	Inclusive Technology	PC	KS1/Adult
A multimedia version of the word building cards, plus visual discrimination puzzles and word searches. It can be used by an individual or with a friend. Particularly useful at home to reinforce spelling work done in school.			

Title	Publisher	Platform	Age
Henrietta's Book of Spells	Lander	Ac/PC	KS2/3
Spelling activities in a storyline setting, with the computer keeping records of efforts. Can also be used for practising French, German, Spanish and Italian words.			
I Can Spell	Resource	Ac/PC	KS1/2/3/4
A variety of spelling games which are fun for children and can be structured to support the necessary teaching for individual children or groups.			
In Sound	JP Innovations	PC	KS1
A form of ILS where pupils are introduced to the activity, provided with a worksheet which they complete away from the computer and come back to check the results. Excellent introduction for children with specific learning difficulties for developing strategies for working more independently with help from the computer.			
Keyspell99	Words Worldwide	PC	KS2/3/4/Adult
Utility to help dyslexics analyse spelling problems and discriminate between homophones.			
Learn More About Words	Inclusive Technology	PC	KS1/2/3
A range of multi-sensory activities including finding missing letters in the alphabet, selecting target word for pictures, about words, spelling the word for picture, word searches, matching word to picture from three beginning with same letter and simple picture crosswords.			
Leximark Spellmasters	Leximark	peripheral	KS1/2/3/4/Adult
DC250 Spellchecker/DC450 Spellchecker/Databank/ DL500 Collins Electronic Dictionary/DC750 Thesaurus/ DT650GB Oxford Children's Spell Corrector. A range of stand-alone spellcheckers. The DC450 has a good range of spelling support plus a calculator and telephone list. The DT650GB has all the features of the Franklin Elementary (including the dictionary book) plus improved error checking, a grammar guide and a protective cover.			
Magic-E	Xavier	Ac/ PC	KS1/2
Computer game for practising changing words by adding an 'e'.			
Making Sense with Words	Inclusive Technology	PC	KS2/3
Multi-sensory activities with groups of words to encourage reading, comprehension, spelling and learning about parts of speech.			
National Literacy Hour	Spellwell	PC	KS1/2
Comprehensive range of spelling activities, with word groups related to the National Literacy Hour lists.			

Title	Publisher	Platform	Age
Oxford Talking Dictionary	Learning Company	PC	KS2/3/4/Adult
	Interactive dictionary with more than 100,000 words and 500,000 definitions; can be accessed while using other applications.		
Penfriend	Design Concept	Ac/PC	KS2/3/4/Adult
	Predictive typing program which provides better support for unconfident spellers than a spellchecker. Also includes an on-screen keyboard with clever punctuation facility and can be used as a screen reader for other text.		
Predictability	Inclusive technology	PC	KS2/3/4
	Simple word prediction program that will speak if you have a sound card.		
Predict IT	Semerc	PC	KS2/3/4
	Full feature word prediction package. Learns the words you use and alters the words offered taking into account the frequency of use by an individual.		
Quictionary Pen	iANSYST	Peripheral	KS3/4/Adult
	A hand-held scanning device that will read and speak out words from (most) books, journals etc. It requires a very steady hand and may not like some fonts.		
Sherlock	Topologika	Ac/PC	KS2/4
	Supportive cloze procedure program with speech prompts to improve spelling, reading and punctuation.		
Soapbox	Xavier	Ac/PC	KS2/4
	Words can be matched by shape and then built up by selecting from a fan of letters. Files of some word families are provided or you can make up your own.		
Starspell 2001	Fisher-Marriott	PC	KS2/3/4
	The latest version of an old favourite which has spoken sentences for each word, onset and rime and extra activities, plus all the Literacy Hour words in groups.		
Superspell	4Mation	Ac/Mac/PC	KS1/2/3/4
	Comprehensive fun environment for learning spelling rules and patterns; contains diagnostic tests in the support materials and photocopiable practice sheets.		
Symbols to Sentences	Widgit	Ac	KS1/2/3
	Runs talking rebus supported reading and spelling activities on the Acorn that were made on Writing with Symbols.		
TextHELP!	TextHELP Systems	PC	KS3/4/Adult
	A utility to run in Windows to provide audio support for text in other programs. Words, phrases, sentences or paragraphs can be selected to be spoken. Also has text prediction and abbreviation facilities.		

Title	Publisher	Platform	Age
THRASS-IT	THRASS	PC	KS2/3
	Designed as IT support for a paper-based scheme for teaching spelling and handwriting. Can be used on its own, but if the child does not already know the THRASS chart, it could be daunting.		
Tray	Letts	Ac/PC	KS2/3/4/Adult
	Updated version of the old Developing Tray/IntroTray programs. Excellent for developing supported awareness of word patterns and spelling.		
WinTray	Letts	PC	KS1/2/3
	Updated version of the old Developing Tray/IntroTray programs. Excellent for developing supported awareness of word patterns and spelling.		
Wordbar	Crick	PC	KS3/4/Adult
	A compact on-screen word facility that helps with spelling and organising phrases for producing reports and essays. It can be used with a full desktop or CE Windows word processors.		
Wordshark2	White Space	PC	KS2/3/4
	A comprehensive, interactive, multi-sensory set of activities in a computer games format for teaching and reinforcing spelling and reading skills. Two sets of wordlists are provided from Alpha to Omega and the Literacy Hour, or you can make your own.		
Wordsquare	SPA	PC	KS1/2/3/4
	Lets you make squares containing hidden words; you can either list the words for the player or they can be given clues for each word.		
WordWorks1	Resource	Ac	KS1
	Word activities for KS1 that can be used with a group in the Literacy Hour or for extra practice, when children work on their own.		
WordWorks2	Resource	Ac	KS2
	Word activities for KS2 that can be used with a group in the Literacy Hour or for extra practice, when children work on their own.		

software to support memory skills

Title	Publisher	Platform	Age
AcceleRead and AcceleWrite	iANSYST, REM	Book	KS2/3/4
	A book providing materials and explaining how to use a talking word processor.		
Mastering memory	CALSC	PC	KS1/2/3/4/Adult
	Designed by speech therapists to help people with memory problems to develop strategies to improve memory. Requires 1:1 support, as strategies have to be discussed.		

Title	Publisher	Platform	Age
ScanIT	Maia Learning Systems	PC	KS2/3/4

Designed to improve reading speed and accuracy. Back-up logging system records progress and increases speed as the pupil progresses. Words, phrases and sentences can be provided in the files, with increasingly subtle distracters, which can be useful for identifying the type of reading errors being made. Useful for developing skills to stay on task.

Tidy (Fun and Games)	H&S	Ac	KS1/2

Excellent program from the Fun and Games suite, for developing short-term memory, sequencing and visual discrimination skills in young children.

Timely Reminders	CALSC	PC	KS4/Adult

Teaches strategies for revisiting, rehearsing and revising material.

software to support cognitive skills

Title	Publisher	Platform	Age
All About Shape and Space	Semerc	PC/Mac	EY/KS1

A multi-sensory activity CD-ROM, exploring the cognitive areas of sorting, matching, sequencing, symmetry, space, right angles and direction.

Chatback	Xavier	Ac	KS1/2/3/4/Adult

Useful for developing auditory discrimination skills or correcting speech difficulties as the child can listen to words or sounds in real speech, record a personal attempt and then check it.

Harrison's Alphabet Book	Moonstone Multimedia	PC	KS1

A simple introduction to the letters of the alphabet for very young children.

IntelliPics	Inclusive Technology	PC/Mac	EY/KS1

Utility for making a wide range of early matching activities.

Jigsaw	Crick	PC	EY/KS1

Jigsaw-generating program for on-screen puzzles of 4 to 42 pieces. Ideal for developing visual discrimination skills. Comes with lots of pictures or you can add your own.

Jolly Post Office	Dorling Kindersley	PC/Mac	EY/KS1

Sorting, sequencing, designing stamps, sending postcards can be practised in a Post Office environment.

Making Tracks to Literacy	Widgit	PC	EY/KS2

ILS

An ILS for young children, where a routeway can be planned through a range of matching, sorting, sequencing, counting and early reading activities. Particularly useful in supporting children with short attention spans.

Title	Publisher	Platform	Age
My World: Copy Match and Sequence	Inclusive Technology	Ac/PC	EY/KS1

Many of the My World screens provide extra rehearsal of early cognitive learning. Some activities help the dyspraxic child to move on to interpretation of information without failing from the frustration of craft activities.

Title	Publisher	Platform	Age
Nursery Rhyme Time	Sherston	Ac/Mac/PC	EY/KS1

Animated traditional rhymes for children to watch and listen to, sing along with, or play with as they wish. Good for early reading related to developing a concept of rhyme.

Title	Publisher	Platform	Age
Point	Advisory Unit	PC	EY/KS1

A utility for providing word and picture banks on an overlay keyboard.

Title	Publisher	Platform	Age
Reader Rabbit Toddler	Learning Co.	PC/Mac	EY

Early skill acquisition in a fun environment that small children can explore independently or as a focus for activities with parents.

Title	Publisher	Platform	Age
Roamer	Valiant	Peripheral	EY/KS1/2

A programmable floor turtle, which can be connected to a computer with an extra attachment. Routes (procedures) can be programmed into it and amended if necessary. Used by young children as a precursor to logo, but planning and implementing routes could be very helpful for developing spatial skills for dyspraxic children.

Title	Publisher	Platform	Age
Sounds and Rhymes	Xavier	Ac/PC	KS1/3

Structured activities for developing phonic awareness, onset and rime as well as rhyming.

Title	Publisher	Platform	Age
Spider in the Kitchen	Inclusive Technology	PC/Mac	EY/KS1

A multimedia approach to learning positions and sequencing.

Title	Publisher	Platform	Age
Talking Animated Alphabet	Sherston	Ac/Mac/PC	EY/KS1

Each letter changes into a character beginning with the same letter name. The child can hear the name and toggle back and forth as much as is needed to learn the letter names.

Title	Publisher	Platform	Age
Talking Rhymes	Topologika	Ac/PC	EY/KS1

Popular nursery rhymes with lines that can be listened to, then sequenced in pictures or words.

Title	Publisher	Platform	Age
Tizzy's Toybox	Sherston	Ac/Mac/PC	EY/KS1

A treasure chest of multi-sensory sorting, sequencing, matching, counting, rhyming, visual and auditory discrimination activities that can be done at different levels. Where explanations are needed, there is speech support.

Title	Publisher	Platform	Age
Book Spinner	Widget	PC	KS1/Adult
Word processor/desktop publishing (DTP) package.			
Claude and Maud	Semerc	Ac/PC	KS1
A fun way of learning how letters are formed and simple spelling. It is used most effectively with a touch screen or a special graphics tablet and stylus.			
Clicker Plus	Crick	Ac/Mac/PC	EY/KS1/2/3
A utility, which provides linked talking word, phrase and picture grids. These can be used on their own at the earliest stages of language development or in conjunction with a word processor. Clicker3 (PC) has its own integral word processor. Grids can be made for any curriculum area and there are several prepared files that can be purchased.			
Fun With Texts	Camsoft	Ac/Mac/PC	KS3/4/Adult
Contains a Concordance program, which replaces the old word-frequency program. Language modules available to enable the user to set up the program so that on-screen instructions are in the target language.			
Handwriting for Windows	KBER	PC	KS1/Adult
A utility for generating text in the exact style a school uses. Useful for making worksheets, handwriting practice sheets in different formats and display labels.			
I Can Write	Resource	Ac/PC	KS1/2/3
A supportive program for generating word, phrase and topic banks to support unconfident writers. Also helpful for helping disorganised writers to plan their ideas.			
IDONS	IDONS	PC	KS3/4/Adult
Planning software for preparing information for essays, reports and revision.			
Inclusive Writer	Inclusive Technology	PC	KS1/2/3/4/Adult
A talking rebus word processor developed for mainstream use from Writing with Symbols 2000. It is useful for weak readers and spellers, especially those with strong visualisation skills, as it enables a link to be made between an image and a word. There is a rebus spellchecker. Rebus support can be progressively reduced as confidence increases. Especially useful for preparing written work at home and printing final work without the rebuses.			
IntelliTalk	Inclusive Technology	PC/Mac	KS1/2
A simple talking word processor that can be used with Intellikeys or Clicker.			
Kid's Designer	Semerc	Peripheral	KS1/2
A simple graphics tablet for drawing or handwriting. Using the stylus with Claude and Maud, can be helpful for a dyspraxic child to get feedback while learning to make letter shapes.			

Title	Publisher	Platform	Age
New Reading Disc	Cambridge Training and Development	PC	Adult
	An interactive multimedia tool for supporting the development of literacy skills in adults. Also useful for writing, and developing study and life skills at KS4.		
Pages	Semerc	Ac/PC	EYKS1/2
	A talking word processor where the text is in boxes that can be placed and/or angled anywhere on the page. This is particularly useful for setting up the labels for talking diagrams, as they can be placed as a list on one part of the page and dragged in to position on the diagram.		
Punctuate	Xavier	Ac	KS3/4/Adult
	Progressive support for teaching and revising punctuation.		
Sassoon Fonts	Sassoon and Williams	PC/Mac	KS1/2/3/4
	An easily read font for using in word processors and/or worksheets.		
StartWrite	Sherston	PC	KS1/2/3
	Utility for teachers to create handwriting worksheets, with letters in dotted script. Variety of font styles to choose and clip-art can be added to pages.		
Storybook Weaver	TLC	PC/Mac	KS2/3
	A multimedia story writing program for children to use for making talking books.		
Talking First Word	RM	PC	KS1/2/3
	A simple version of Word, available at three levels with speech support and included in RM Windowbox software.		
Talking Pendown	Logotron	Ac/PC	KS1/2/3
	Talking word processor with talking wordlist facility.		
Talking Textease	Softease	Ac/Mac/PC	KS1/2/3
	Multi-sensory multimedia word processor. Text is placed in a box, which can be placed anywhere on the page, so especially useful for making talking worksheets with talking labels for diagrams.		
Talking Write Away	Semerc	PC	KS1/2/3
	Configurable talking word processor designed for use with children.		
TalkWrite	Resource	Ac	EY/KS1/2
	A talking word processor that can include pictures and pre-prepared animations to make lively worksheets or can be used with wordlists to support the child's own writing.		
TextHELP!	TextHELP Systems	PC	KS3/4/Adult
	A utility to run in Windows to provide audio support for text in other programs. Words, phrases, sentences or paragraphs can be selected to be spoken. Also has text prediction and abbreviation facilities.		

Title	Publisher	Platform	Age
Write:Outloud	Don Johnston	PC/Mac	KS2/3/4/Adult
A talking word processor with many supportive features including a talking toolbar, the spellchecker from Franklin Spellmasters and a button for inserting pictures.			
Writer's Toolkit	SCET	PC/Mac	KS2/3/4/Adult
A supportive program for developing writing for particular purposes.			
Writing with Symbols	Widgit	Ac/PC	KS2/3/4/Adult
A rebus word processor, which can be used to make talking rebus supported materials on the (Acorn) computer and printed out as rebus supported text.			

software to support numeracy skills

Title	Publisher	Platform	Age
123 CD	Sherston	Ac/Mac/PC	EY/KS1
A multi-sensory approach to learning about the early stages of number skills.			
Amazing Maths	CSH	Ac/PC	KS1/2
A multi-sensory approach to practising basic numeracy skills, set in a maze environment. Particularly useful where spatial awareness is a problem.			
Animated Numbers	Sherston	Ac/Mac/PC	EY/KS1
Bright, clear introduction to numbers and simple counting; uses overlay keyboard.			
Cars – Maths in Motion	CSH	Ac/PC	KS2/3/4
A cross-curricular approach through racing cars, including planning, decision making, reading and calculations, which could provide motivation for some de-motivated learners.			
123 CD	Sherston	Ac/Mac/PC	EY/KS1
A multi-sensory approach to learning about the early stages of number skills.			
ClickSheet	Crick	Ac	KS1/2/3
This is an extension to Clicker (for Acorn only) to provide a maths processor environment to facilitate number work. Very useful for supporting the learning of place value.			
Clockwise	4Mation	Ac/Mac/PC	KS1/2/3
A range of time and date activities, on different clock types, which can be made progressively difficult. Includes life skill activities of setting an oven timer and estimating time and an adventure game.			
Clockwork	Resource	Ac/PC	KS1/2
An attractive program for younger learners to become familiar with or rehearse learning about time.			

Title	Publisher	Platform	Age
First Logo	Logotron	Ac/PC	KS1/2
Simple, supportive logo program; dragging the pointer to a new position on the screen gets the program to provide the commands in the procedure window.			
GoGo	Semerc	Ac	KS1/2/3
A simple supportive logo program with on-screen buttons and procedure windows to support children with spatial awareness problems.			
Graph Plot	Semerc	Ac/PC	KS2/3
Simple data-handling program, where information can be quickly and easily displayed in different graph formats; ideal for enabling the dyspraxic child to move to the 'What if...?' stage in maths work more rapidly than if graphs have to be hand drawn.			
Inside Track Maths	AVP	PC	KS4
Model GCSE papers and answers, which students work through on paper and check back with the computer. Teachers can monitor progress and prepare customised papers.			
Interactive Calculator	Inclusive technology	PC/Mac	KS2/3/4/Adult
A multimedia calculator designed to provide supported and progressive learning of how to use a calculator, including a 'guesstimate' button and a tracking system for the teacher.			
Junior Pinpoint	Longman Logotron	Ac/PC	KS1/2
Simpler version of Pinpoint, a data-handling tool. Questionnaire design is flexible to set up and easily modified and data can be entered to form database and graphs. Helpful for dyslexic children to learn how to organise/sequence ideas.			
Learn More About Maths	Inclusive Technology	PC	KS1/2
Multimedia practice and reinforcement activities, covering counting to 9, sequencing numbers, pelmanism, time, adding and subtraction to 12. Good for young, non-reading children or older pupils who have problems with basic maths skills.			
Letts GSCE Maths Revision Guide	Letts	PC	KS4
Support for revising GCSE maths.			
Math Blaster/Junior	Adventure	PC/Mac	KS1/2
Opportunity to practise numeracy skills in an arcade environment. Different games for different levels.			
Mathmania	Topologika	Ac/PC	KS2/3/4
Maze environment with number, shape and space, time and measurement obstacles that can be configured for difficulty.			

Title	Publisher	Platform	Age
Maths Book	Topologika	Ac/PC	KS1/2/3
	Supportive maths processor to help layout and understanding of place value; especially useful for dyspraxic pupils who have difficulty with layout and dyscalculic pupils who have problems with the basic concepts of numeracy.		
Maths Circus	4Mation	Ac/Mac/PC	KS1/2/3
	Problem-solving maths in a circus environment, involving logic and sequencing; can be done by trial and error, so it encourages pupils to discuss how they got there. Keeps records for the teacher and also has paper tasks.		
Millie's Math House	Iona	PC/Mac	EY/KS1
	Multimedia cartoon-style early concepts activities, to make maths fun for young children.		
My World: Fractions	Semerc	Ac/PC	KS1/2/3
	Activities to provide extension and reinforcement practice where the child has co-ordination difficulties.		
My World: Maths	Semerc	Ac/PC	KS2/3
	Number activities to provide extension and reinforcement practice; especially useful where the child has co-ordination, number reversal and sequencing difficulties.		
Number Shark	White Space	PC	KS2/3
	An extensive range of games that can be configured to provide support for acquiring numeracy skills in a supportive, competitive environment. The child's efforts are logged and the competition is against their own results.		
Numbers Disc	Cambridge Training and Development	PC	KS4/Adult
	This disc was designed to support adults with numeracy problems, but could be useful for older pupils.		
Numbers You Need	Cambridge Training and Development	PC	KS3/4
	A series of CD-ROMs covering decimals/fractions/ percentages/approximation and estimation/negative numbers/games, supported with a tracking program to record progress. The emphasis is on real-life situations and there is good use of speech and animations for support.		
Screen Turtle	Topologika	Ac/PC	KS2/3
	This turtle program is tolerant of some spelling, use of upper/lower case in procedures, so allows less confident users to have success more easily than some logo programs.		
Sheetwise	Semerc	Ac/PC	KS1/2/3
	Simple introduction to spreadsheets.		
Spider and Friends	Inclusive Technology	PC/Mac	EY/KS1
	Multimedia early number activities.		

software to support numeracy skills (continued)

Title	Publisher	Platform	Age
Table Aliens	Sherston	Ac	KS2
Four arcade adventures with tables activities which can be customised for tables used, speed of shooting and length of game.			
Talking Clocks	Topologika	Ac/Mac/PC	KS1/2/3
Telling the time and differences in analogue and digital clocks, supported with speech.			
Time and Fractions	Xavier	Ac	KS1/2
Structured programs designed for supporting dyslexic problems with many options and levels and good graphics.			
What Do You Do When You Can't Learn the Times Tables?	Semerc	PC	KS3
Provides you with some ways to learn the times tables facts. A range of strategies are provided for pupils to experiment with.			

software to develop keyboard skills

Title	Publisher	Platform	Age
Big Keys (qwerty)	Semerc	Peripheral	KS1
A simplified qwerty keyboard for use with young children. It has large well-spaced letter and number keys, limited access extra functions and can have lower or upper case labels.			
Concept Universal Plus	Semerc	Peripheral	EY/KS1
The Concept keyboard was vital in providing word bank support on older computers. It has been somewhat superseded by on-screen grids, but some younger users still find it more meaningful to touch the words or pictures on an overlay.			
Fingers for Windows	APT	PC	KS4/Adult
Typing practice with sound support; can be used with foreign languages too.			
First Keys to Literacy	Widgit	PC	KS1/2/3
Designed for teaching young children the keyboard layout, this can also be used to develop reading and spelling skills in a structured way. There are many sample files and graphics to use straight away, and it is easy to tweak existing files or make your own. KS2 and even KS3 children enjoy using it if the files are adapted.			
Intellikeys	Semerc	Peripheral	EY/KS1
An overlay keyboard that can be used to supplement, or replace, a conventional keyboard. It is useful for young children to use with wordbanks or pictures and words together. Comes with a range of overlays and software to make your own customised materials.			

Title	Publisher	Platform	Age
Kaz	Future	PC	KS3/4/Adult
A typing training program that uses special sentences to teach the layout. It can be helpful for some dyslexic users but confusing for others.			
Kid's Ball	Semerc	Peripheral	EY/KS1
Some young children, or those with co-ordination problems, find it easier to use a trackerball than a mouse. The access device stays still in a suitably placed position and can be operated with two hands. There are several makes, but avoid the ones where the ball can be lifted out of the casing!			
Light Bytes	Summerfield Publishing	PC	KS2/3
A simplified version of Keybytes, which is a program for teaching IT skills. Could be useful as more motivating keyboard reading material for encouraging reluctant readers, but at present it is not possible to get the material read by the computer. It could be a useful tool for parents to use with their child to improve their own IT skills.			
Mavis Beacon teaches typing	Mindscape	PC	KS2/3/4/Adult
A comprehensive typing trainer, including video on seating etc.			
Roller	Penny and Giles	Peripheral	EY/KS1
A large trackerball with a facility to lock the select button to drag items. This is useful for young or poorly co-ordinated children, as the device stays still in a suitably placed position and can be operated with two hands.			
Speedy Keys	Semerc	Ac	EY/KS1
A lively approach for young children to match letters on the screen with those on the keyboard.			
Touch Type Read & Spell	Computer Course	PC	KS2/3/4/Adult
Keyboard training scheme linked in to developing reading and spelling skills; suitable for adults as well as children.			
Touch Type Tutor	iOTA	Ac/Mac/PC	KS2/3/4/Adult
Typing training supported with real speech prompts. Detailed analysis of key presses so it is possible to see which keys are not yet well known.			
Type to Learn	TAG Developments	PC/Mac	KS2/3/4/Adult
Typing training with links to spelling and punctuation. Levels of words used can be chosen. Includes a word processor. Goals are automatically adjusted as progress is made.			

appendix b: software suppliers

developers of software
mentioned in the text

ABC CD: talking animated alphabet
Sherston Software Ltd

Book Spinner
Widgit Software Ltd

Claude and Maud
Granada Learning/SEMERC

Clicker
Crick Software Ltd

CoPS Baseline Assessment
Chameleon Assessment Techniques Ltd

Co:writer
Don Johnston Special Needs Ltd

Crosswords
Software Production Associates (SPA) Ltd

Developing Tray
London Educational Technology
Support Service (LETSS)

Encarta Africana
Microsoft Ltd

En Route
Granada Learning/SEMERC

Expression
Scottish Council for Educational
Technology (SCET)

Eye for Spelling
LDA Multimedia

Fun with Texts
Camsoft

Gamz word search
Inclusive Technology

Inclusive Writer
Widgit Software Ltd/Inclusive
Technology Ltd

Inspiration
iANSYST Ltd

Interactive calculator
Inclusive Technology

Keyspell
Words Worldwide

Magic-E
Xavier Educational Software Ltd

Mastering memory
Communication and Learning Skills
Centre (CALSC)

My World 2
Granada Learning/SEMERC

Naughty stories
Sherston Software Ltd

Numbershark
White Space Ltd

Oxford Reading Tree talking stories
Sherston Software Ltd

Predict IT
Granada Learning/SEMERC

Prophet
Ace Centre Advisory Trust

Rainbow stories
RESOURCE

**Sherlock: the case of the
missing text**
Topologika Software

Talking Pendown
Logotron

TextHelp!
TextHELP Systems Ltd

ThinkSheet
Fisher-Marriott Software

Timely Reminders
Communication and Learning Skills
Centre (CALSC)

Touch-type, read and spell
Philip Alexandre Computer Campus

Wellington Square
Granada Learning/SEMERC

**What do you do when you can't
learn the times tables?**
Granada Learning/SEMERC

Wordbar
Crick Software Ltd

Wordshark 2
White Space Ltd

Wordsquare
Software Production Associates (SPA) Ltd

Wordswork
iANSYST Ltd

Write:outLoud
Don Johnston Special Needs Ltd

addresses of developers

ACE Centre Advisory Trust
92 Windmill Road
Headington
Oxford
Oxfordshire
OX3 7DR

Tel. 01865 763508 01865 759800
Fax 01865 759810

info@ace-centre.org.uk
www.ace-centre.org.uk

Cambridge Training and Development
43 Clifton Road
Cambridge
CB1 4FB

Tel. 01223 582582
Fax 01223 585551

Camsoft
10 Wheatfield Close
Maidenhead
Berkshire
SL6 3PS

Tel. 01628 825206
Fax 01628 825206

100611.671@compuserve.com

ourworld.compuserve.com/homepages/
GrahamDavies1/

Chameleon Assessment Techniques Ltd
Staythorpe
Newark
Nottinghamshire
NG23 5RG

Tel. 01636 646719
Fax 01636 646718

info@chameleon.org
www.chameleon.org

Communication and Learning Skills Centre (CALSC)
131 Homefield Park
Sutton
Surrey
SM1 2DY

Tel. 0181 642 4663
Fax 0181 642 4663

info@calsc.co.uk
www.calsc.co.uk

Crick Software Ltd
1 The Avenue
Spinney Hill
Northampton
NN3 6BA

Tel. 01604 671691
Fax 01604 671692

info@cricksoft.com
www.cricksoft.com

Don Johnston Special Needs Ltd
18 Clarendon Court
Calver Road
Winwick Quay
Warrington
Cheshire
WA2 8QP

Tel. 01925 241642
Fax 01925 241745

jmunro@djsn.u-net.com
www.donjohnston.com

Fisher-Marriott Software
58 Victoria Road
Woodbridge
Suffolk
IP12 1EL

Tel. 01394 387050
Fax 01394 380064

sales@fishermarriott.com
www.fishermarriott.com

Granada Learning/SEMERC
Granada Television
Quay Street
Manchester
Greater Manchester
M60 9EA

Tel. 0161 827 2927
Fax 0161 827 2966

semerc.sales@granadamedia.com
www.semerc.com

iANSYST Ltd
The White House
72 Fen Road
Cambridge
Cambridgeshire
CB4 1UN

Tel. 01223 420101
Fax 01223 426644

sales@dyslexic.com
www.dyslexic.com

Inclusive Technology
Saddleworth Business Centre
Delph
Oldham
Greater Manchester
OL3 5DF

Tel. 01457 819790
Fax 01457 819799

inclusive@inclusive.co.uk
www.inclusive.co.uk

LDA Multimedia
Abbeygate House
East Road
Cambridge
Cambridgeshire
CB1 1DB

Tel. 01223 357788;
01945 463441 sales
Fax 01223 460557

ldaorders@compuserve.com
ldamarket@aol.com

Logotron
124 Cambridge Science Park
Milton Road
Cambridge
Cambridgeshire
CB4 OZS

Tel. 01223 425558
Fax 01223 425349

info@logo.com
www.logo.com

London Educational Technology Support Service (LETSS)
The Lodge Crown Woods School
Riefield Road
Eltham
London
SE9 2QL

Tel. 0181 850 0100
Fax 0181 850 0400

letts@compuserve.com
www.letss.com

Microsoft Ltd
Microsoft Campus
Thames Valley Park
Reading
Berkshire
RG6 1WG

Tel. 0345 002 000
Fax 0870 602 0100

www.microsoft.com.uk

Philip Alexandre Computer Campus
PO Box 535
Bromley
Kent
BR1 2YF

Tel. 0181 464 1330
Fax 0181 313 9454

101322.343@compuserve.com
http://www.ttrs.co.uk/index.html

RESOURCE
51 High Street
Kegworth
Derby
DE74 2DA

Tel. 01509 672222
Fax 01509 672267

info@resourcekt.co.uk
www.resourcekt.co.uk

Scottish Council for Educational Technology (SCET)
Dowanhill
74 Victoria Crescent Road
Glasgow
G12 9JN

Tel. 0141 337 5000
Fax 0141 337 5050

enquiries@scet.com
www.scet.com

Sherston Software Ltd
Angel House
Sherston
Malmesbury
Wiltshire
SN16 0LH

Tel. 01666 843200
Fax 01666 843216

info@sherston.co.uk
www.sherston.com

Software Production Associates (SPA) Ltd
PO Box 59
Tewkesbury
Gloucestershire
GL20 6AB

Tel. 01684 833700
Fax 01684 833718

sales@spasoft.co.uk
www.spasoft.co.uk

TextHELP Systems Ltd
Enkalon Business Centre
25 Randalstown Road
Antrim
County Antrim
BT41 4LJ

Tel. 01849 428105
Fax 01849 428574

info@texthelp.com
www.texthelp.com

Topologika Software
1 South Harbour
Harbour Village
Penryn
Cornwall
TR10 8LR

Tel. 01326 377771
Fax 01326 376755

info@topolgka.demon.co.uk
www.topolgka.demon.co.uk

White Space Ltd
41 Mall Road
London
W6 9DG

Tel. 0181 748 5927
Fax 0181 748 5927

sales@wordshark.co.uk
wordshark.co.uk

Widgit Software Ltd
102 Radford Road
Leamington Spa
Warwickshire
CV31 1LF

Tel. 01926 885303
Fax 01926 885293

literacy@widgit.com
www.widgit.com

Words Worldwide
Ash House
Belle Villas
Porteland
Newcastle upon Tyne
NE20 9BE

Tel. 01661 860999
Fax 01661 822777

Info @keyspell.com
www.keyspell.com

Xavier Educational Software Ltd
Psychology Dept
University of Wales
College Road
Bangor
Gwynned
LL57 2DG

Tel. 01248 382616
Fax 01248 382599

xavier@bangor.ac.uk
xavier.bangor.ac.uk

larger educational software suppliers

This list indicates some of the larger educational software suppliers who are able to offer a range of titles. For additional information, refer to the Educational Software Database, which is maintained and managed by Becta. This database contains information about thousands of software packages which are educational in nature, available in the UK and targeted at the pre-school to further education market. The database can be found at:

http://vtc.ngfl.gov.uk/resource/esr/

ABLAC Learning Works Ltd
South Devon House
Newton Abbott
Devon
TQ12 2BP

Tel. 01626 332233
Fax. 01626 331464

www.ablac.co.uk

AVP
School Hill Centre
Chepstow
Monmouthshire
NP6 5PH

Tel. 01291 625439
Fax. 01291 629671

avp@compuserve.com
http://www.avp.co.uk/

Cambridge CD-ROM Ltd
Coombs Tannery
Stowmarket
Suffolk
IP14 2EN

Tel. 01449 774658
Fax. 01449 677600

sales@cambridgecd.co.uk
http://www.cambridgecd.co.uk/

Cumana
Whitegate
Dunmow Road
Hatfield Heath
Bishops Stortford
Hartfordshire
CM22 7ED

Tel. 01279 730900
Fax. 01279 730809

sales@cumana.co.uk
www.cumana.demon.co.uk

Granada Learning/SEMERC
Granada Television
Quay Street
Manchester
Greater Manchester
M60 9EA

Tel. 0161 827 2927
Fax. 0161 827 2966

semerc.sales@granadamedia.com
www.semerc.com

iANSYST Ltd
The White House
72 Fen Road
Cambridge
Cambridgeshire
CB4 1UN

Tel. 01223 420101
Fax. 01223 426644

sales@dyslexic.com
www.dyslexic.com

Inclusive Technology
Saddleworth Business Centre
Delph
Oldham
Greater Manchester
OL3 5DF

Tel. 01457 819790
Fax. 01457 819799

inclusive@inclusive.co.uk
www.inclusive.co.uk

Matrix Multimedia Ltd
10 Hey Street
Bradford
West Yorkshire
BD7 1DQ

Tel. 01274 730808
Fax. 01274 730808

sales@matrixmultimedia.co.uk
http://www.matrixmultimedia.co.uk/

Rickett Educational Media (REM)
Great Western House
Langport
Somerset
TA10 9YU

Tel. 01458 253636
Fax. 01458 253646

info@r-e-m.co.uk
www.r-e-m.co.uk

RM plc
Marketing Department
Akzo Buildings
135a Milton Park
Abingdon
Oxfordshire
LX14 4SE

Tel. 01235 826000
Fax. 01235 826999

salesdesk@rmplc.net
http://www.rm.com/

TAG Developments Ltd
Dept PR101
25 Pelham Road
Gravesend
Kent
DA11 0HU

Tel. 01474 357350
Fax. 01474 537887

sales@tagdev.co.uk
www.tagdev.co.uk